Charlotte E. Nixon Payne

A Pacifist in Time of War

Charlotte E. Nixon Payne
Her Diary and Stories

Compiled and first transcribed by her daughter,
Rhoda E. Lawrence
1951

Re-transcribed and edited by her grandson,
C. Meyrick Payne
2020

ISBN: 978-0-9701374-5-6 (paperback)

Book Design by Cheryl Mirkin

For information write to:
Management Practice Inc.
216 West Hill Road, Suite 200
Stamford, CT 06902
www.MFGovern.com

Table of Contents

Contents

Essays

1919–1948

Essays

Poems

Preface by C. Meyrick Payne, Charlotte's Grandson, 2020

'The responsibility of the oldest generation is to pass on family stories"

After a brief preface, issues for discussion, family tree, an anthology of her funny poems, Charlotte's transcribed diary is written in chapters. Her exploits, stories about Charlotte from her family, and essays are interspersed between chapters. Her war time poems are transcribed at the end of the book.

Charlotte was a most remarkable woman, a Pacifist and Suffragette, well before her time.

I have come to know Charlotte through her diary and research into her life. I remember meeting her once in 1950 when she was living with her daughter Rhoda in Essex England. I had previously met her when she visited my parents Basil and Betty in Roslyn, Long Island in 1948 and again in Greece in 1949, although I have no memory of those occasions.

Her life's journey and accomplishments are impressive. She was a strong woman, before her time and probably difficult to live with because of her passionate convictions, especially when her husband and children were intimately involved in the war effort. In many ways she was proven right by history.

She believed that women should have political power, but she was infuriated when women, who had so much to lose, refused to speak up about the folly of war.

Her childhood was fascinating; growing up in the late 19th century in an upper middle-income family. She aspired to marry well. She was adreamer, a romantic and passionate about everything; All of this is well recorded in her diary.

Her side story, Minor Key, is, I believe, about her great romance beginning in 1904. In Switzerland she met a man who died of tuberculosis in
1906. Although there is no written evidence, my mother Betty told me that
Charlotte talked to her about this time. Charlotte also gave my Mother a
silver cutlery chest, from the top of which had been hacked a family crest,
which my Mum believed to have been that of her lover's family. Minor Key
is, I believe, secret code to conceal her first unrequited love.

Perhaps on the rebound, but determined to find a suitable, interesting
match, Charlotte married my Grandfather Meyrick in 1907. Like Charlotte,
Meyrick was musical, literary and witty but more practical. They had her
first daughter, Iris, in 1908. She left Iris in the charge of nannies, while she
went to join her husband in the Sudan, Africa. The diaries reveal that she
hated her experience there.

She returned to England and probably embarked on a European adventure, which she writes about in her story Kindred Soul. Again, there is no
direct evidence, but the timing of events makes it likely that this was in
her adventure.

Her first protests were against the Boer War in South Africa in 1902.
She felt this war was brought about by the colonial, and nationalist, am-
bitions of Britain, France and The Netherlands. World War One was, in
her opinion, entirely unnecessary, and the result of a family spat between
Queen Victoria's children and grandchildren. She hated war, but she hated
war time propaganda even more. She could never forgive the politicians,
press, church and misguided women for hiding the Truth from the people.

Throughout her diary she spells Truth with a capital T.

She writes about her love for her children. She strives to protect them
from the savagery of war. She describes the marriage of her daughter, Rhoda
in 1935. In just one sentence she reveals that her husband Meyrick walked
out of her life on that same day. He never received another mention.

Perhaps her only reference of her loss, was a short poem she wrote:

"I must contrive
To keep alive
All through 1935,
For 1936 may be
The best year of eternity."

No gnashing and wailing for Charlotte – but just a touch of sadness and regret.

Her protest lacked its pinnacle during WW II. She hated Churchill and his wartime propaganda. She regularly protested at Speakers' Corner in London, where British people have always gathered to advocate their controversial points of view.

In 1942 her Naval officer son Basil married Betty, also a Naval officer. They shortly began a family. She hated the idea of bringing children into a war-torn world.

Daughter Rhoda recalls a fascinating story about Charlotte's protest placards falling from a cupboard in front of her husband's armament manufacturer colleagues. Very embarrassing!

Immediately after the war, Basil joined the United Nations, in part to placate his Mother. A couple of years later, Charlotte came to New York where she learned to love my Mother. The following year Charlotte travelled to Greece where Basil was then stationed with the UN.

In 1950 a seriously ill Charlotte went to live with her daughter Rhoda in Essex. She stayed until her death in 1951 at the age of 72.

Charlotte was a talented, kindhearted but determined woman, many years ahead of her time.

Stamford, CT 2020

Acknowledgments

First and foremost, I am grateful to my Aunt Rhoda, Charlotte's daughter, who first transcribed the diary and provided many of the stories about her mother. Aunt Rhoda also provided one of the few original diary hard copies, upon which this book is based.

Belinda (Mindy) Brooks, my cousin and Charlotte's granddaughter. provided many insights and inspired many wonderful discussions.

Verity and Brian Thornton, also cousins and grandchildren, helped to edit the proofs. They also documented the Payne, Nixon, Brooks, Wells and Lawrence family tree, which provided 265 names and email addresses for Charlotte's descendants.

Richard Wells, a great grandson, found over 100 edits and corrections including research into Charlotte's story that her grandfather Horacio Stopford Nixon, fought at the Battle of Trafalgar.

Anthony Payne, Charlotte's husband Meyrick Whitmore's nephew, provided insight into the successful musical and poetic collaboration between husband and wife.

Special thanks to my wife, Donna Tatroe, who married into this sprawling clan, and put up with my obsession to pass Charlotte's story onto future generations.

Thank you all

Issues for Discussion
Concerning the Life of Charlotte Nixon Payne

1. How do you feel about being a Pacifist in time of war?

2. Is her view of Churchill in any way justified? For her is there a "just war"?

3. How do you feel about war time propaganda? Why did she spell Truth with a capital "T" throughout her diary?

4   Is Charlotte a poor little rich girl striving to improve her lot in life?

5   Charlotte never received a formal education, yet she was smart, did that hold her back?

6. Was Charlotte tough to love? Why did her husband leave on their daughter's wedding day?

7. Was Charlotte anti- Semitic? Why do you think so?

8. Did Charlotte marry her husband, Meyrick, on the rebound?

9. Was Charlotte a romantic? Or a pragmatist?

10. Why did Charlotte not write about the holocaust in her post war essays? About the 1918 Spanish 'flu? About the great depression?

11. Did her son, Basil, really join the UN after the war to placate his mother?

12. Why did she write her love story, Minor Key, as a secret document?

13. Do you think Charlotte, while newly married with a baby, went on a secret European adventure (as in Kindred Soul)?

14. Did Charlotte's adventures predetermine the activities of her descendants?

15. How will history view Charlotte?

Charlotte Nixon Payne Family Tree

As of August, 2020

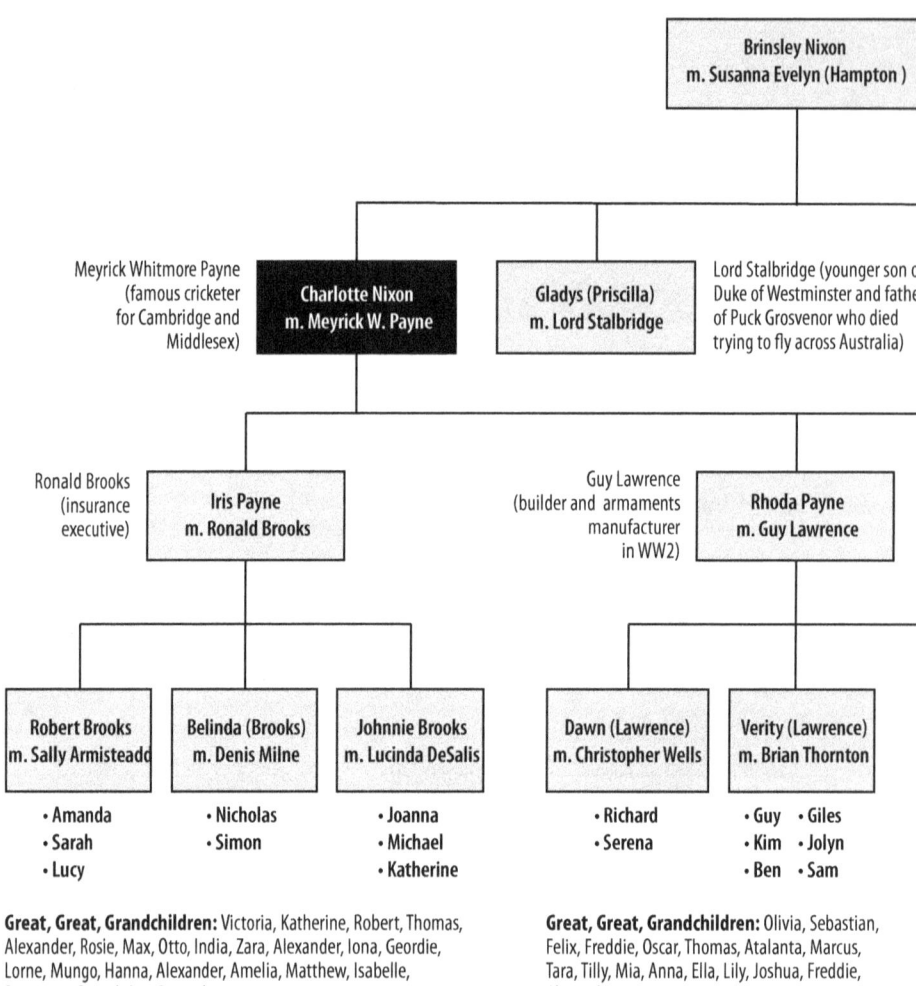

Great, Great, Grandchildren: Victoria, Katherine, Robert, Thomas, Alexander, Rosie, Max, Otto, India, Zara, Alexander, Iona, Geordie, Lorne, Mungo, Hanna, Alexander, Amelia, Matthew, Isabelle, Benjamin, Daniel, Joe, Samuel

Great, Great, Great, Grandchildren: Isla, George, Albert, Ada

Great, Great, Grandchildren: Olivia, Sebastian, Felix, Freddie, Oscar, Thomas, Atalanta, Marcus, Tara, Tilly, Mia, Anna, Ella, Lily, Joshua, Freddie, Alexander

Parents: Brinsley and Susanna Evelyn Nixon

Grandparents: Horatio Nixon, and Thomas and Elizabeth Hampton

Aunt: Isabelle and Henryk Wieniawski (famous Polish Violinist)

Niece and Nephew: Irene Wieniawski and Sir Aubrey Dean Paul (known as Strawberry)

Great Niece: Brenda Dean Paul (famous socialite, actress and drug experimenter)

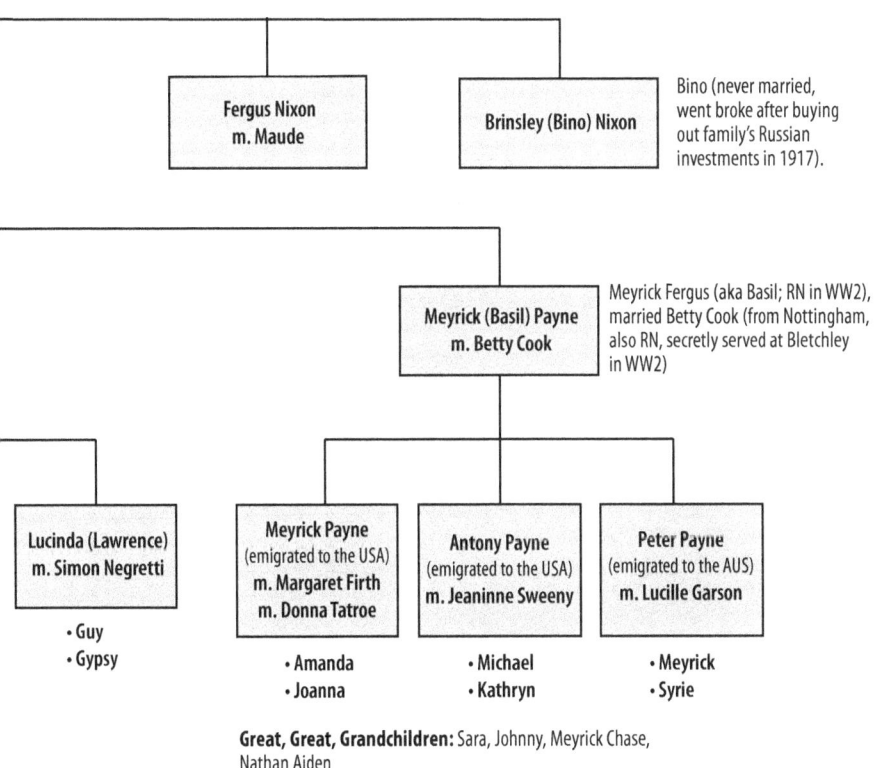

Fergus Nixon
m. Maude

Brinsley (Bino) Nixon

Bino (never married, went broke after buying out family's Russian investments in 1917).

Meyrick (Basil) Payne
m. Betty Cook

Meyrick Fergus (aka Basil; RN in WW2), married Betty Cook (from Nottingham, also RN, secretly served at Bletchley in WW2)

Lucinda (Lawrence)
m. Simon Negretti

Meyrick Payne
(emigrated to the USA)
m. Margaret Firth
m. Donna Tatroe

Antony Payne
(emigrated to the USA)
m. Jeaninne Sweeny

Peter Payne
(emigrated to the AUS)
m. Lucille Garson

• Guy
• Gypsy

• Amanda
• Joanna

• Michael
• Kathryn

• Meyrick
• Syrie

Great, Great, Grandchildren: Sara, Johnny, Meyrick Chase, Nathan Aiden

Charlotte's Poems: She Can be Funny Too

Explanatory note by CMP. Throughout her diary Charlotte rails against the folly of war. She was a classic pacifist and believed deeply in women's suffrage. Her diary entries and related essays are replete with her battle cry for justice and Truth about war. But she was also funny with a witty streak which played well in her social circle. Here are a few of her more amusing verses. Her more serious war time poems are at the end of this book. They are well worth reading.

Poem: The Bridge Friends (Card Games with Friends)

Cutting and shuffling all their narrow days,
Living for pasteboard scattered on green baize.
They talk Bridge, hink Bridge
Eat Bridge, drink Bridge
Smell Bridge, stink Bridge,
Until through endless dreams of Kings and Aces,
Flabby as Knaves become their foolish faces.

A moon-faced girl I know named Mabel,
Married a goof across the table,
He felt, in spite of all the trouble,
Friendly towards a chance to double
It did not take Love long to pall
His "two hearts" was an over-call.
The first time that they went to bed,
Let's have a game my dear," he said
Her answer took him quite aback
"Yes, tell me dear, do you have a pack"?
"I wonder, can we raise a four?"
"Ring up and ask the Browns next door."

Although slightly hurt at her "no bid,"
Obedient to her call, he did.
The Browns had turned in for the night
But, being friends, they came all right!
And this went on till all were dizzy
And Mrs. Brown had lost a tizzy,
(It was the limit she'd afford,
And she didn't like the way they scored).
So, then they tried just as a pair
But this was more than she could bear.
For playing all night double dummy,
Sadly, upset poor Mable's tummy.
No sooner would they start to doze
Than he or she with screams arose.
They'd leap from sleep, with terror start,
 "I double! Pass! No, one heart!"
They'd groan and toss the sheets away,
"You doubled! Why? For God's sake, why?"

Poem: Golf (dedicated to my husband)

A friend, I'll call him Sam for short,
Is one of those the bug has caught
Though studying books by expert's writ
For those bereft of brain or wit.
His game at last has grown so bad
It drives him (and his partners) mad.
He toddles daily round the links
Twice, between copious rounds of drinks.
The someone tells him, the silly clown,
It is his clubs that let him down.
So off he goes and spends a lot on
Buying a set by Henry Cotton.
And aided by his latest curses
His game gets infinitely worse.

And then this pest, who anyway
Absents himself throughout the day,
Homeward returns at eventide
To one who, thank God, never tried
To undermine her mental balance
Or prostitute her natural talents,
Knocking a ball to make it roll
Into a silly little hole.
And then he tells her missing none,
Of every hole he should have won.
And she, poor dear, must hide from Sam
She simply doesn't give a damn!

But medal days are much the worst
For her, a period accursed,
If he should win t'will only mean
Another cup for her to clean.
Some useless little tinpot prize
That puffs him up to twice his size.
And if he loses, she must lie
All the dismal night long, hearing why.
If one thing's certain, it is this,
The fault is never never his.

Perhaps the caddy was to blame
That staggering urchin with his load,
Who lagged behind him as he strode,
Who coughed just when the moment came,
While God and Nature stood stock still
For fear he'd even miss the pill!
Was it the caddy or some bird?
She said, "who made the noise you heard?"
"I do not know" he nattered, "but
Somebody **made** me miss the putt."
And near the dawn, her saddened eyes open wide
Upon the stentorian idiot at her side.
Oh, Golfers' wife I offer thee

For what it's worth, my sympathy.
God give thee power, (until divorce)
To live, be good and stay the course.

Poem: A Prayer (The Danger of Bike Riding in a City)

O Point Policeman,
Thou whose hand
Can bid the roaring traffic stand.
When swirling motors pinch and press
Missing me by an inch or less.
O help me, low and humble like.
Who ride in peril on a bike.

Poem: A Lyric (A View of Love, which Dies So Easily)

Love is the thing on earth
Best living for.
You ask what is it worth?
The best thing on earth?
Red roses seem to be
One emblem we see
Showing love's worth.
Flawless, sensuous, red,
Deep-hearted roses.
Their fumes mount to the head,
Love seeks a scented bed.
Roses and love die soon
Both on a summer's noon
Shewing love's worth.

Poem: Another Lyric (Of Nature's Omnipotence)

And God said: "Let there be light"
And the world was lit by
Golden beams, silver gleams
The radiance of sun and moon.
By the glimmering stars at night
The shimmering heat of noon,
Glittering iridescence
Of oceans, rivers, streams.
A luminous quintessence
Of Nature's myriad schemes,
A miracle world – white – shining
For men's creative dreams.

Poem: To June (The Dream Time of the Night)

The garden lay a dreaming, in the silver sheen of night,
The glimmering stars and moonshine shone down translucent light.
A mystical, still radiance, sensuous accents of summer night,
The garden steeped in silver peace, celestial and white,
In this glamour, cuckoos clamour, fluted calling in the night,
In the fragrance of syringa and the jasmine scented night
In the floodlight of the moonshine, in the dream time of the night

Poem: Tides (Murmurous Roar Breaking on the Shore)

The lovely sound of waves upon the shore
Unending, murmurous roar.
That breaks the silence of unspoken thought
Unending rhythm find unending sound
Tumultuously the waves break on the ground
Of rocks and sand,

And fill the vast horizon with their song,
Crashing, splashing, breaking on the shore
Unending, murmurous roar.

Poem: To Sleep (Come Sleep and Be Unending) (Charlotte's Last Poem Before She Died in 1951)

Veils of sleep come drifting deep, mystical and magic sleep
Veils of sleep enfold me, submerge and enshroud and hold me,
All good we know will pass in death
And end the right to happiness.
Veils of sleep come stealing, the consciousness from feeling
Cloud the senses and the heart, the tumultuous rebel heart.
Come sleep this life transcending, come sleep and be unending.

CHAPTER ONE

Family Background, Childhood and the Death of Her Mother 1879–1889, Aged 1–10

"The minority is always right."

This is the dictum of wisdom, but how disastrously it has failed!

Possibly the flaws in its technique may become obvious if I write my autobiography because, although a woman of no importance, I have consistently been placed in environments in which I found myself a minority of one.

Heredity plays its part, so one must write prehistory, the lives of one's parents and what they stood for. My father, Brinsley de Courcey Nixon, was a descendant of the family of Nixon of Fermanagh and Cavan. He lived with his mother in Edinburgh.

She was a Scotswoman. His father, Horatio Stopford Nixon, who was Irish, had been in the Navy and was Captain on the Bellerophon* at the Battle of Trafalgar.

He died of cholera when my father was six years old, his mother's brother, William Fergus, lived at Kirkaldy, next door to Edinburgh, and

---

* Richard Wells, Charlotte's great grandson, and a scholar of the Battle of Trafalgar, could find no definitive record of a Nixon at the Battle. However Charlotte was convinced he was there.

Charlotte Aged Four

my father worked in his business. William Fergus was a Liberal and represented his constituency at Westminster for many years. He was unmarried, and it was understood that my father would be his heir when he died. However, it was found that his liabilities exceeded his assets.

Reading through the diaries which my father kept meticulously throughout his life, one realizes how gay Edinburgh was in those days. There are many accounts of Adare and Lissadel in Ireland where he constantly stayed. When he was twenty-eight his mother died. Her death was a terrible grief to him.

The house in Edinburgh was sold and he went to London and started a business career there. He was fortunate in some ventures and, in the course of years, became a rich man. Shortly after his mother's death he stayed with his Irish cousins in the South of France. There were five sisters, all very good looking.

Seafield at Westward Ho, North Devon

The youngest, Jessie was probably the most beautiful and he became engaged to her. The date for the wedding in Cannes was fixed and then my father went back to London for a few days. On his return, he found her ill with typhoid. This illness ended her life.

Two years later he married her sister and they had many years of happiness together. For some unknown reason, she was a chronic invalid and died when she was comparatively young.

When my father married my mother, she was twenty-five and he was twenty-five years older. She was very lovely, very witty and had great musical talent. She was Irish and, like my father, a rebel and unorthodox. Both under the influence of Huxley, Tyndall, Haeckel and Ingersoll. He considered orthodox belief in the resurrection of Christ and Life Everlasting to be disastrous to the interests of humanity. They believed, as most

3

Charlotte Aged Seven

of us do today, in the teaching and example of Christ, the goodness of God and man's duty to make heaven on earth.

My father was a Liberal. He stood twice for Parliament; once for Dundee, where he stood against Hicks Beech but failed to be elected. The chief accusation leveled against him by the Conservative opposition being that he was an atheist. In the course of time there were four children of which I was the eldest.

Life should have been pleasant for my mother for she adored her children, had adequate money, a house in London and one in Seafield, which she had influenced my father to build on the North Devon coast. There must have been a vein of irresponsibility in her character, or possibly she thought so much for and about other people, that she failed to think about herself.

She was fragile and she neglected her health, ruined her digestion, eating practically nothing, and fell back on stimulants. Her constitution was undermined and when she had a serious illness – influenza developing into pneumonia and jaundice she died. Possibly also, the doctors may have made a mistake and not given her the best chance; in serious illness, there is so little division between life and death.

The worst thing had happened. A hopeless vista stretched before us, because children who lose their mother are at a terrible disadvantage.

A box came this morning for me from Devonshire with a lovely lot of flowers in it and some cream from Mrs. Passmore and after that we had raffling in fathers' hat. I got a lot of jewels out of the cracker that they filled my jewel box.

July 30, 1886. Friday 8th Birthday. Seafield, North Devon

When I was dressed, I went to see nurse and baby and I could see baby in his bath. After that I had my presents and then after that I bathed. In the afternoon Godfrey came and we stayed in the garden and played a game of croquet and then we had tea. In the evening, we went for a drive in the mule cart. After that we came home and danced.

January 1, 1890. London

The new year opens with a thick fog and finds 27 Collingham Gardens a sick house. Us children all down with whooping cough. Mother and Father both bad with colds. Lussy recovering from peritonitis. Sissy Hoare also down with whooping cough and Minnie with rheumatic fever.

April 10, 1890. Seafield

It is a frightful day, pouring with rain and the wind is howling and wailing around the house. We are miserable. Mumskins is very sick and ill. Dr. Acland came. This afternoon went to the post office. Stayed with mother. Doctor came again and slept here all night.

April 11, 1890

Much finer today and mother much better. Stayed with mother all morning as the others went out. This afternoon we all went to Bideford and bought presents for mother. Coming back, we went to the station and welcomed Nurse Stone. Doctor came. He said mother was much better. Priscilla (later Gladys Stalbridge), Fergus and I went on the rocks.

April 13, 1890. Mumskins Birthday

Glass fallen; weather terrible but Mumskins better. We all went into Mother 's room to see her have her presents:

A ring from Father
A pair of vases from Mad
Vases from Priscilla
A pair of vases from me
A view and ornaments from Fergus

Doctor came. Parry sent us some flowers, I arranged them. This afternoon we all went on the cliffs. Bino threw his hat over the cliffs.

May 7, 1890. London

Very fine day today. Went to school. Packed up odds and ends.
This is my diary and so I shall put what I think in it. Nobody need look in it and if they do, they must not think it improper!
Through that beastly Mademoiselle's untruths which she wrote in her letters, Mother has resolved to send me away from home. I have promised

to be good until next Wednesday but if I don't come back in a week, I won't say any more. Went to my new school with Lussy and mother to Mrs. Passmore, 22 Gordon Place, London where they have left me to my fate; did lessons.

April 3, 1891. Seafield

Fergus and Edward went to the links; I went to the tuck (sweet) shop. Afterwards Lussy and I went to see Mrs. Pool. We found her crying dreadfully, as her little girl Christian had fallen into the baths yesterday and drowned. She was only two and a half years old. I went up with Lussy to see her and she looked so lovely.

May 24, 1891. London

Mother is very ill. We are very anxious about her.

June 15, 1891

Not a very nice day. Mother is just the same and we are all very unhappy. Went to school and did lessons. When we came back mother was said to be much better. Father let Lussy take us to the Crystal Palace for the Exhibition. We went in the arenas. Me and Priscilla rode on the switchbacks.

June 26, 1891

I sent in an essay on roses to the New Yorker and I won the prize!
Darling mother who is much better was delighted with it. Went to church. Stayed at the garden.

June 30, 1891

Did not go to school, Mother had a restless night and though not sick she is fearfully weak. At 11 o'clock we all went in to see dearest Mother. We all kissed her, and she recognized us. She patted Fergus and Bino on the head and said "This is my big boy, and this is my little boy."

July 1, 1891

The doctor has told us all that there is no chance of mother getting better. I sat in her bedroom. She, dearest little mother, is quite unconscious and looks so ill.

July 2, 1891

Darling dearest little mother (Mumskins) (Wifekins) left us this morning between 7:30 and 8. Dearest was quite unconscious, but we heard her moaning: Oh, fearfully.

July 4, 1891. London

Dearest Mother was cremated.

July 13, 1891

It is a very fine day and we have all gone back to School to start everything again and to go on as before only with one great difference, our mother is gone.

"For we must work, as well as weep and the sooner it's over the sooner to sleep.

And the harbour bar goes moaning."

CHAPTER
TWO

School and Teenage Stories
1890–1897, Aged 11–18

Death is an incomprehensible shock to children. We adored our Mother who was so lovely and attractive and of whom we were so proud. We lived in a welter of unhappiness and my sister and I were quite pleased when the doctor, a few days after mother's death, ordered surgical operations for us.

The months of anxiety about her illness had reduced us to a state of debility in addition to which was the fact that it was July and we had three dusty months at the High School. I had glands on the side of my neck, and Priscilla was supposed to have adenoids. In her case I am sure, it was an unnecessary operation There was no suggestion made of getting into better condition in country air, and the operations took place at home.

In the middle of August, we went down to Seafield, but the magic of summer seas had gone and the beauty of blue and gold seemed to make one even more miserable.

One day in September just before our return to London, we were glooming by the front door when a large party of the very young people came towards us. Two or the girls we recognized as school friends. Their brother was with them and one of his Cambridge friends. They came to tea and afterwards we went down to the rocks.

The boys were amusing, and we found ourselves laughing. It was a crescendo of laughter and we were so out of practice it seemed our laughter must have creaked like unoiled hinges. After that, as always happens, time placed strata upon strata of events upon remembrance until gradually our irretrievable loss was buried under the weight of happenings and life became normal again.

Our nursemaid governess Lussy (Miss Lennard), had become our house-keeper. She was a kindhearted woman but had little education. I do not think anyone was particularly interested in our well-being. My father had been an only child and, not acquired a family until late in life, he had little experience of children.

Christmas Day, 1891. Collingham Gardens, London

A black fog, the streets like sheets of ice. After having given our presents to father, Lussy and the servants, we went to the school room and found on the table a box of crackers from the servants. A book each from Luster, a frame with mother's photo in it, from Priscilla, a box of sweets each from Bolton, and to Priscilla a book from me.

My mother's sister occasionally came over from Brussels and brought her two daughters to stay with us. Her husband had died many years previously – he was the great violinist, Henrik Wieniawski. Irene, the youngest daughter, inherited his genius and we had wonderful music, Irene playing the piano and Tootza, the violin.

Our London house was gay and spacious and light streamed in. A conservatory on the first floor was filled with palms, ferns and flowers. The routine was orderly, even the clocks were wound once a week by a visiting clock-man.

Before my Mother's death l had learned the contrast to live poor, and it was a punishment.

Priscilla, Bino and I returned from Devon to resume schooling. A French governess, who had come for the Easter Holidays, was still in charge of us.

A great many children lived in our gardens and after tea on those Spring evenings we gathered to play the most uproarious and intriguing games of "French and English." We looked forward to this medley with great enthusiasm.

On this evening, we must have transgressed for Mlle. Bonard told us that as a punishment we had to stay in. Argument was of no avail. Some other means had to be found. We maneuvered ourselves out of the schoolroom and, closing the door, I turned the key firmly in the lock and took it away. Immediately there was clamour.

Mademoiselle rang bells, and screamed orders to surprised man-servants to fasten and lock the back-stairs door and the front door to prevent our escape. We had not hurried and were unprepared for this development, but our independence was still assured because the whereabouts of the missing key was unknown to them.

Men servants stood on guard at the front door and at the top of the back stairs. Priscilla, Bino and I went to the dining room. The windows were open (there were window boxes) and a basement. These, however, were not to defeat us. Grimly we got out of a window and, at some risk, holding on to iron railing, we achieved our liberty. We had a wonderful time that evening in the gardens and, later, with dignity, I let Mademoiselle out of the schoolroom.

I was punished afterwards for this incident and was sent to Mrs. Rayner's who lived on the north side of Kensington High Street, with her daughter, Faith, who was the same age as myself and who went to the High School.

It was a dismal house on a dismal street, and, although clean, it was dark and depressing. The only points in its favour being that it was close to Kensington Gardens and contained well stocked book shelves, I was quite resigned about it all and it was only when I found myself back at home for some reason that the contrast bore overwhelmingly on my conscience.

At home, there were peonies and lilac everywhere and the lovely light and air streaming in everywhere. I must have effectively made my protest because my trunk was sent for. I did not return to Mrs. Rayner.

Subsequently, two winters after my Mother's death, there was the incident when I was expelled temporarily from High School. It happened to be the day of a great occasion. Royalty on the platform and a march past of the whole school. We were arrayed in our gym suits – dark blue Jersey with a red sash round the waist and tied in a bow at the back – the girls marched two abreast down the middle of the hall, up to the platform, bowed to the Great Ones, divided sharply left and right returning in a single file and leaving the hall.

When it came to my turn the two red sashes in front had intrigued my sense of humour. I tied them together, with the result that, turning sharp left and right, the two girls, nonplused and stood mystified and spellbound.

Overcome with merriment, I cannot remember whether anyone else joined. I omitted to bow to Royalty and slunk down the left side of the hall. Later that day my disgrace was underlined. The Headmistress told me that I must leave the School and that she was writing to my father.

A hansom cab and acid faced mistress were in attendance to see me home. When the driver set off in the wrong direction I objected, but was told to be silent; consequently, we were driven half way round Kensington before we reached Collingham Gardens.

Father was out, thank goodness.

I opened and read the letter before giving it to him that evening. The headmistress and he must have reached a reasonable conclusion. Shortly afterwards I returned to school.

Life was lived at slow tempo, no motors, telephones, radio or even bicycles.

One term Priscilla and I contracted ringworm. It is a disgusting disease. Our doctor seemed unable to cope with it or cure it.

Then we were sent down to stay with Lussy's sister who had a small house on the outskirts of Bognor Regis. She was an irresponsible person, but quite unsuitable to be given the charge of children.

In her living room I found and read, Bocaccio's Decameron, which was unfortunate literature for a girl of fourteen. Existence in that house meant nothing to do and nothing to think about – a sheer waste of time.

It is essential in the years between thirteen and sixteen, when energy is super abundant that time should be disciplined by wholesome intellectual activity and good physical exercise. Sensuality then remains dormant.

At seventeen one reaches the romantic age and is on the road to heaven!

I must have been nearly sixteen when I went to Roedean, a great school. Its founder Pauline Lawrence ("PL"), was one of the worlds great women.

Standards were all good, and time disciplined. Unfortunately, I was only there for five terms and then Priscilla, who hated the school she was at in London, decided to come to Roedean. My father could not be left without a daughter.

It was years later then looking through my father's papers that I read a letter PL had written telling him that for me to leave Roedean and not finish my education was a definite mistake. She urged him not to allow me to do this and said that later I should go to university.

PL, of course, did not understand that our domestic difficulties which right at that time seemed insurmountable. So, Priscilla, who had been more or less expelled from her very select school in Queen 's Gate, owing to complete lack of concentration and interest in learning, went down to Roedean. I went back to London to act as hostess for my father.

May 1896. *London*

Directly after breakfast, I went with father to the stores where we ordered invitations for our debutante dance and visiting cards for me.

Drove home in a hansom cab. After lunch, Priscilla and I went to Humphrey's to give my dress a final fitting. My word, trying on is decidedly fatiguing, Priscilla giggled inanely the whole time. The whole establishment appeared to have some hand in my costume, and Mr. Humphrey, on coming in to see how it looked on, decided to alter the whole style. I know I shall not like it now.

It is much too fussy. Ordered a perfectly sweet opera cloak.

June 9, 1896

First dance, first season, at home.

All day preparing for dance in the evening and consequently feeling a bit tired by the evening. We all assembled in the drawing room by 9:30 pm, a lovely array of beauty, rank and fashion. The Thompson boys arrived first and afterwards everyone else trooped in; what a fearful squash.

Got dead tired introducing the guests. Everyone looked very nice at the start but looked rather like wrecks at the end of the evening. Kept it up until quarter to four!

London, January 1897

Went to Maud's with Jem and Priscilla. Sybil and I went and had our fortune told by palmistry. Well, you never knows, your luck.

This is the horoscope of Charlotte Evelyn Nixon as told by the palmist at Hereford Lodge, S W London.

"Queen of change and sudden wild excitement of action, strife and revolution in whom is the spirit of Pallas, Athene and Mars.

At the hour of your birth there were curious portents. The moon, ruler of the Ascendant, is found in exact conjunction with the lover of strife and action. The great Mars, the giver of energy, and close to these two is Mercury, the mental ruler, in conjunction with the cursor of sudden mysterious and romantic changes. the potent Uranus.

With this collection, your soul will be like a stormy petrel. You will delight in change and excitement. If ever in your life there are social upheavals, like the French Revolution, you will be a leader like Madame Roland.

You will marry prosperously, a man rich and probably older than you, in good social position and with lands, and you will gain in social position by the marriage. You will have money but be extravagant and hate losses. Your children will inherit your love of excitement and action and your liability for accidents. This year will be a very happy one, especially about the middle of June next year. "

I was depressed because, although seventeen, I was under sized, barely five feet tall. Possibly I would have grown taller, but owing to ignorance, I did things that probably hindered growth. I wouldn't drink milk. I wore long boned corsets, tightly laced and high-heeled shoes and had, as a background, a home where there were so many things to look after. By this time, I had acquired a very strong sense of responsibility.

It seemed it was my primary duty to look after my family owing to the fact that there was no one else to do it. So Father enjoyed entertaining and in those days hospitality was lavish, large dinner parties where fourteen, eighteen, or twenty people sat down to perfectly cooked food and good wine, seven or eight courses, the table glowing and glittering with flowers, fruit, candles sparkling glass and silver. A fairy layout followed by two hours of genial conversation and no sign of digestive impotence.

Priscilla the previous year had been seriously ill with an attack of acute rheumatism. We had gone down to Seafield at Easter time and a week after her arrival the illness started. Looking back, it is possible her bed, unaired had reeked with moisture.

This attack affected her heart and she seemed excessively fragile. Lussy at this time had an acute attack of rheumatism, probably from the same cause. As a tonic the doctor ordered her champagne. This was unfortunate as from that date her sobriety was unpredictable.

My father suffered from chronic neuritis and was on a special diet which was supposed to effect a cure.

My experience is that damp, any form of damp, is the main cause of rheumatism. I have had lumbago from sitting in a car in which a wet waterproof or a wet dog had just vacated; tennis elbow from driving a car in which rain penetrated on that right side and frostbite from wearing wet boots continuously throughout the day – for this last and chilblains, Philip's rubber soles on all shoes is the cure and preventative.

With the provision of well aired beds, Seafield was the perfect health house. Built on rock on the rim of the Golden Bay, filled with ozone from the Atlantic tides, it had a narrow strip of garden from which a path ran down to the pebble ridge and rocks.

From these rocks a swimming pool had been blasted, which was concrete lined, with iron stairs embedded in its sides to carry ropes. This pool was probably our salvation, the danger of the Golden Bay, being that there are no boats, only fishing smacks over the Bar, on the other side of the bay. As it was our pool had been made especially for us, we felt it incumbent to swim there.

In a house a few yards down the road lived children of our own age, and whenever possible we played the super game of Follow My Leader, in plimsolls. It was a mad pastime jumping from rock to rock at the edge of the sea and resulting often enough, in cut knees and shins and, occasionally, falling into deep water from which we emerged dexterously.

Then there was Paradise, a lovely cleft between the hills opposite Seafield. In springtime it was filled with bluebells and primroses and violets, and later, with hawthorn, dogross and honeysuckle. What a wonderful fragrance it seemed in those days.

At the top of the valley we found a little cave roofed by hawthorn trees and here we brought rugs and books and felt isolated and superior This was when we were very young.

Later, in more sophisticated years, I was sitting one morning high up in the valley looking down on a rough sea when I saw two dots in the water.

It seemed they were in trouble. I watched but there was nothing I could do at that distance. Then I saw the approach on the sands of one or two other dots who swiftly joined those in the water, and in time all were back on the sands together.

It was Priscilla and a friend caught in a horrible ground swell. They could not get back and both being small, were practically out of their depth. If it had not been for the approach and courage of two tall American friends who hauled them out in time, they might have been swept out by the tide and drowned.

Priscilla and my youngest brother, Bino, were foolhardy. They took unwarranted risks and caused endless anxiety. One summer day we arrived at Hartland Point for a picnic. I was unpacking the luncheon basket when calm was shattered by news that Priscilla was stuck on the cliffs and could not get up or down.

Swiftly coastguards with ropes appeared. I remember looking over one of the highest and most precipitous cliffs to see Priscilla cowering beneath an overhanging ledge only a very short distance from the top. She was hauled up and, thank God, no lives were lost.

When Bino was at Cambridge he acquired a minute dinghy. It was adrift at the edge of the rocks but was not seaworthy. He and my sister used to paddle right into the middle of the Bay, miles out, till they became specks in the distance. I used to listen to the rising wind and watch the oily looking breakers foaming on a smooth sea, and I often cursed their crass stupidity.

Luck must have been with them for they always got away with it although the boat, generally full of water, sank before reaching shore.

CHAPTER
THREE

Coming Out and First Boy Friend
1898–1899, Aged 19–20

"If your Morals make you dreary, depend upon it they are."
When Priscilla heard that I was going abroad she decided to come too and left Roedean College. We went to Monte Carlo, Bordighere and the Italian Lakes. It was all very lovely!"

Sunday 24, June 1900

At 12 pm we all started by the funicular up to the Rocher de Neige. Such a glorious day. At the hotel, we had a most excellent lunch and then went up. Father also, to the most extreme point. Sat down, gasped and admired the view. It was perfectly gorgeous.

On one side, range upon range of perfect snow-capped mountains, with just a glimpse of Mont Blanc behind one of the peaks most distant from us. On the other the deep, precipitous valley with glorious blue Lake Geneva stretching out for miles beneath. Father, Priscilla and Auntie Bella returned by train. Fergus, Nurse Sharp and self, walked. Scrambled would perhaps be the correct term, for it proved to be the most trying and dangerous descent. However, we lived to tell the tale. Had tea at Caux and sauntered into the hotel in time for dinner.

Priscilla was ill with bronchitis at Bordighere and I succumbed Lumbago with a sore throat which the doctor said was diphtheria, but it was not. When we got back and were sitting down to a very good dinner, Father said it was necessary to go abroad to realize how much better everything was at home.

In the following year, we had our "coming out" ball. In those days to enjoy dancing one had to have space and a superlative floor; also, of course, the best band. The dance took place at Connaught Rooms. A crowd was invited, and a crowd came. They all seemed good lookers, both men and girls. There were more men than girls. Everyone seemed to enjoy themselves and, in the months, that followed there were dances and parties of every description.

Priscilla was the prettiest girl that anyone had ever seen. Her photograph appeared in a series called "Types of English Beauty." She was small, but taller than me by two or three inches, had wonderful dark blue eyes, black lashes and a mass of brown hair. She was very like our mother, only her hair had been golden. Unfortunately, she remained delicate and doctors said her heart was weak.

Most of our cousins were in the Army or Navy. In those days, the Services seemed the best medium for an enjoyable life. We went to Sandhurst, Woolwich and Greenwich to dance with them, and we watched them play polo at Hurlingham and Ranelagh. My eldest brother, Fergus, was going into the Amy. He was seventeen and cramming for Sandhurst.

A friend brought a Major Chetwynd to our "coming out" ball. His regiment was at Folkestone and, during the following months, he and his friends contributed considerably to our entertainment. He was very good looking and very many years older than me.

From the sentimental point of view, I was an impossible proposal proposition being entirely preoccupied in running the house and looking after my father and Priscilla and generally in the grip of anxiety complex.

At the end of that summer the Hussars were leaving for India. To my great surprise, the Major asked me to marry him. He wrote such a charming letter and made the proposition sound so attractive that I was conscious of hesitation, but I was, not in love and there was a temperamental barrier – or I thought there was – music, which to me was a primary value, was outside his interests.

I must have written an indefinite reply because he joined the train on which my brother and I were traveling back from Scotland and came down to Seafield with us. It was only a two-day visit, and I saw him off en route for India. As he stood leaning out of the train window, Hugh said "If, instead of going to this accursed India, I could have stayed here a few more months, I could have made you marry me."

"Very possibly" I thought, but I was feckless. At nineteen life's endless road stretched before one. There was plenty of time. Duty seemed plain. I was needed at home. however, I answered his letters for many months.

Then the South African Boer war broke out. The symmetry of existence and military leave from India was canceled.

At Seafield, three years later, a day's golf had finished. We were sitting after tea reading the papers, the room gilded with the light of the setting sun, I read the obituary notice of Hugh Chetwynd.

He had died at Lucknow of typhoid. I went out of the room, out of the house, climbed the hills, and then over fields on top of the hills, and then went down into a valley of gorse and heather.

The sea glinted in the distance. I sat down on the pungent turf and remembered things, things forgotten, unimagined, unsaid, and I had a feeling of responsibility. He had said that if I would become engaged to him, he would not go to India.

Death, being the last word, leaves one forever in the wrong.

CHAPTER
FOUR

Boer War in South Africa
1900–1902, Aged 21–23

"**E**verything has been said to show the obscene folly of war as a medium of settling disputes."

In Tolstoy's "War and Peace" and Bertha van Suttner's "Lay Down Your Arms" the stupidity is written. Everything has been said to show the obscene folly of war as a medium of settling disputes. Unfortunately, people are selfish and do not imagine the sufferings of others. Truth is painful, and consequently they call commercialized murder a Holy Crusade.

Father had made a considerable amount of money in the gold mines of South Africa. He was a director of many South African companies and among our friends were quite a few South African millionaires. They lived in great opulence. Gold streaming in from South Africa was adding to this country's prosperity.

Suddenly the newspaper clamored about the wrong of the Uitlanders. They were overtaxed. It all seemed very unimportant to me. Then, Joseph Chamberlain bristling with pomposity, Milner verbose and one realized that Chamberlain had sent a quite undeserved and dangerous letter to Kruger, the Prime Minister of South Africa. There was talk of sending troops overseas.

The next day, or the following one, I read the answer that Kruger sent.

It was reasonable and dignified. Kruger offered to withdraw armed burghers of his Republic from the borders and suggested that H.M. troops now on the high seas, should not be landed in South Africa and that points of mutual difference should be regulated by the friendly course of arbitration, or by whatever peaceable means might be agreed upon by his Government and H.M. Government.

Then followed preposterous clamour: a howl of jingoism. It must have been, as always, an organized press effort. The only word one could distinguish was 'prestige', and then, the British Government, calling Kruger's letter an ultimatum. British troops were landed in South Africa.

My sense of justice was outraged. I failed to understand how responsible statesmen could act in this way. "War is the bankruptcy of Statesmanship."

My father had the greatest admiration for the Liberal tradition, for Colden, John Bright and Gladstone, but he was against Home Rule for Ireland. Following Joseph Chamberlain, he had become a Liberal Unionist. I never heard him say a word in favour of war, but his loyalty continued in support of Chamberlain.

Ruskin says that when war starts women should wear black and all amusements, theaters etc., should end. Unfortunately, this does not happen, and war becomes an excuse for additional amusement. In the South African war, men did not come back on leave, but London evenings were very gay – the hub of the universe; amusement and frivolity continued.

I went to a dance that first spring. It was given by a South African millionaire: fancy dress, but many of the boys in uniform. We had a dinner party at home. I was dressed as "Night" and considered the whole success of my costume centered on an electric light in my head-dress.

Unfortunately, just before we were due to leave for the dance, the light extinguished itself and I had to wait for an electrician to fix it. The boy who waited with me had earlier been my host. He was now in uniform and going to the Transvaal in South Africa.

He was frivolous about the war and would not take it seriously. He lived to the end and heard the armistice declared then, fantastically, was shot by an explosive bullet. His leg had to be amputated from the thigh and, when he regained consciousness, he died. I read the letter he wrote to his mother before the operation. It was all consideration for her.

Paul Rubens was with us the night of that dance. He is the only person I can remember who danced with me during those years. The dance was at Hyde Park Gardens. Driving back in the early hours, the gates of Kensington Palace Gardens, where Paul lived, were shut and it was with considerable anxiety that we watched him scale over the top.

I was called a pro-Boer during those years, but when facts were assessed by history, everyone became pro-Boer.

CHAPTER FIVE

Older Men and European Travels
1903, Aged 24

"Don't expect happiness in this life, everything is disappointment."

Mrs. Skeffington was leaving the hotel. She had finished her cure. I was sitting beside her in the hall. Perhaps she thought I looked vulnerable to future menace. We stood up to say 'good-bye'.

Although old, she was very good-looking – white hair, eyes glowing with life's intensity, figure streamlined. I thought how beautiful she must have been through the years, and yet she was speaking from experience and had meant what she said, "don't expect happiness in life; everything is disappointment."

Father and Priscilla had come to Aix by doctor's orders. I had come for a change of scenery. Aunt Evelyn was company for my Father and our butler, Sharp, who had been with us for many years, looked after Father and valeted for him.

It was luxury living, planned for the age of wealthy victims of rheumatism, cafe complet in the sitting rooms, then, during the morning, Father and Priscilla proceeded to the baths, carried there on litters shielded from the public. I probably read French novels and arranged roses, which were in profusion, in our rooms.

Déjeuner was at twelve thirty, and afterwards, when Priscilla and father took their prescribed siestas, I would go across to the Casino and listen to the orchestra. Later we would drive to La Bourget or some other lovely place for tea.

If we remained in Aix there was Rumplemayers, its gardens, creme Viennese and strawberry tarts, and in the town, every conceivable luxury shop. I wanted to improve my French and enjoyed talking to an old Hungarian Jew. His face was intellectual and his expression sardonic. He gave me large boxes of Marquis chocolates but unfortunately the ardor of his temperament cooled, and the chocolates and conversations faded out.

We met a Mr. Wormold and he fell in love with Priscilla. It was unfortunate because he was a quarter of a century older than her. He was a great character and personality, extremely generous, but selfish. He was like a spoiled child who had always had everything he wanted. He travelled back to England with us and had with him his valet-courier.

This courier was invaluable to Mr. Wormold whose temper was vitriolic. He had the greatest contempt for all foreigners of whose language he knew not one word. Ramillies, the courier, had arranged all details of the journey when in Paris, but we found that, although our name was on the window of a reserved carriage, it was already filled with people.

Persuasion was attempted with absolutely no result. The occupants sat firm. Porters became increasingly garrulous, I saw Mr. Wormold almost apoplectic with fury. He was mopping his brow and appeared prepared to forcibly eject them himself.

"So, help me, God" he appealed to the Deity as was his habit in an emergency "these blasted foreigners shall be punished for this."

Fortunately, at this moment Ramillies reappeared with the station master and another important looking official. They bowed obsequiously to Mr. Wormold who towered in righteous indignation over them. In a few minutes the interlopers were firmly dealt with, order restored, and we packed into our reserved compartment.

The following winter we went to Cap Martin, a miraculous transition from the depressing grime of London and raw dampness of the English winter. To find oneself in that glistening atmosphere of sunshine, flowers and glittering sea, orange and mimosa trees, was glorious. I remember thinking what folly it was to be in England when this was happening all the time. Mr. Wormold joined us. He had now become part of the family circle.

Another friend, Eric Henderson, came over too. He had been in the war and his right arm had been amputated. He was, of course, in love with Priscilla. I cannot think why in modern parlance; she did not fall for him. Two girls were staying at our hotel. They were the most beautiful, exotic creatures with enormous, black-lashed, gray eyes, creamy skins and perfect figures and just above medium height. The eldest girl fell in love with Eric and they eloped.

Explanatory note by CMP and as recalled by Charlotte's daughter in law. Soon after writing these diary entries, Charlotte met her first true love in Switzerland. He had tuberculosis and lived at a sanitarium close to Davos. She devotes an entire section of her diary entitled, "Minor Key" to recount her relationship. She used the mysterious title to conceal the extent of her first love from her husband and children. Minor Key was only discovered by her daughter Rhoda after Charlotte's death in 1951.

Charlotte and Her Sister;
A Truly Strong Bond

Reminiscences based on stories told to CMP.

Charlotte was the oldest of four siblings, Priscilla (who we knew as Gladys, or Aunt Glad or more formally Lady Stalbridge), Fergus (married to Maude) and Bino (the naughty lad of the family).

All Charlotte's siblings are much mentioned in her diary, but none more so than Priscilla to whom she was devoted.

Priscilla was both admired and envied. She married into one of the greatest families in Britain, the Grosvenor's, which is the family name of the Duke of Westminster. Lord Stalbridge was one of the younger sons, perhaps grandsons, of the Duke, as such he was bestowed with a grand title and considerable wealth, but no great fortune. Her principal residence was Motcombe in Dorset, which is now a school.

Priscilla set a high bar for her older sister. Charlotte records in her early diary a desire to marry well. Alas Charlotte's big love seems to have been Osmond, a codename, who was dying in a tuberculosis sanatorium in Switzerland. This affair seems to have derailed Charlotte's matrimonial plans. Perhaps on the rebound, Charlotte quickly married my grandfather, Meyrick Whitmore Payne and became pregnant with Iris.

Charlotte describes events in Priscilla's life with consistency. Oddly, Charlotte writes little about her husband or her children or even Lord Stalbridge. Instead many pages are taken up with Priscilla's dogs, birds, and housekeepers.

In contrast Charlotte does recall stories about Priscilla's son Hugh (known as Puck). Puck was a grand adventurer and his biography is well recorded. He died attempting to fly his small plane across Australia, where Puck served as aide-de-camp to the Governor General, a truly prestigious position for a young man at the time.

Puck was in line to inherit great wealth from his Grandfather the Duke.

Alas that went up in a cloud of dust. Unfortunate, perhaps because Grosvenor Estates is one the largest property owners in the world today.

Priscilla outlived Charlotte as a widow living near Brighton. I remember visiting her with my parents when I was about 9. She served chocolate pudding for sweet desert. I thought it looked so good that I asked for a double portion. Well, it tasted horrible. I asked for the sugar bowl. My Dad told me that the pudding was sweet enough. I replied, too loudly for my own good, that the sugar would kill the taste. Bad move!

STORIES

MINOR KEY: PART 1

Meeting Her Love in Switzerland
1903, Aged 24

A Confidential Diary by Charlotte E. Nixon.

The year was 1903, and the place the most tragic town in Switzerland. Consumptives or all nationalities came to Davos to cure.

On a hotel veranda, a man and a girl lounged in deck chairs and enjoyed sun saturation. The girl had only arrived three days previously from England. The man was curing. It was his third year at the hotel. He lost weight steadily. He was tall, over six foot and very thin. His hair, auburn, almost red, he had freckled skin and grey eyes, a very sensitive face, the expression of which was generally sardonic.

The girl was small, she had nice grey eyes, freckled skin and the same type of sensitive face. In fact, facially there was a strong resemblance between the two. They might well have been taken for brother and sister.

"What made you come out here?" asked Osmond Wynne.

"I didn't come," answered Lynda (assumed to be pseudonym for Charlotte) petulantly. "My much older traveling companion, John Vickers brought me. I thought we were on our way to Vienna. Suddenly in Paris he changed his mind and took tickets for this drab spot."

John said it was to give me pleasure because I like skating, but John's old friend, Webb, was here and that is probably the explanation.

"And why are you traveling with John Vickers"?

"It is long story" replied Lynda, "He was in a very bad state when my sister married another man instead of him. John was altogether too gloomy. This trip is really a diversion for him."

"Well" replied Osmond "You'll probably enjoy yourself, even here."

"No. It's disappointing. I wanted really to travel. I've been static at home too long looking after other people, particularly my father."

"And now you have freedom?" asked Osmond.

"Yes, absolutely no one to look after, thank heaven and now I have the wanderlust. It should be amusing seeing the world."

"Quite, but looking back on my travels, England and Ireland – more especially Ireland, were soul-satisfying. Unfortunately, it's too late for me to see the world." Osman mused.

His grey eyes met grey eyes, Lynda's questioning his logic.

"No," repeated Osmond almost defensively, "I've nothing to regret. This life has been worth-while."

"Well, has your life been absolutely perfect?" queried Lynda "Yes, perfect," affirmed Osmond.

"Are you, burning the candle at both ends?" Lynda pushed.

"Yes, that is exactly what I am doing" replied Osmond.

"I wonder," said Lynda.

They were the same age and had read the same books, Tolstoy, Wynwood, Read, Shaw; they even thought along the same lines.

They nearly had the same sense of humour.

Both considered music a primary value. Poetry came second and, probably, cricket third. Cricket, in those halcyon days, was important. People took cricket seriously.

They also took life seriously, no damned pantomime, and little sophistication. All Europeans, even Germans, were good Europeans and one loved one's neighbor as oneself.

Osmond's mother had died when he was sixteen and his father, a very eloquent preacher and popular clergyman. He was so immersed in showing people the right road to heaven that he had little time for anxiety, especially concerning the wrong roads his own children might take.

When all is said and done if you are a sincere cleric, orthodox in thought and believe all that you teach, what matter earthly mistakes. Why worry about a short life, even truncated by tuberculosis, if an eternity of heaven lies ahead?

Lynda's childhood had also been marred by that most disastrous loss of a parent. Her mother had died before she was thirteen. Her father, a banker and director of various business concerns, was a man of great integrity. He had a first-class mind and an absorbing passion for Truth. Influenced by Darwin, Ingersoll, Ingersoll and the other great men of that period, he gave his intellectual energy unsparingly to show the fallacy of orthodox religious doctrine.

It was a coincidence that both their fathers were equally sincere and lived within a stone's throw of each other in London. Apparently, they had once met at a small intimate dinner at a neighboring house, but there is no record of their mutual reactions.

Osmond wrote music, and, influenced by religious environment, chiefly for the organ. A good musician can attain celestial heights. He wrote songs. The essence of his lyrics were the poems he chose.

Osmond played these to Lynda. He dedicated his songs to Lynda. He also gave her the Oxford Book of Verse so she could appreciate his poetry.

One night there was an orchestral concert. Osmond secured one of the few luxurious sofa seats running alongside the concert hall. Osmond scanned the programme.

"Dull," he observed, "I don't appreciate Mozart."

Lynda agreed, but at the end Osmond said the piece had been beautiful, even miraculous. Lynda had thought so too.

Christmas and the hotel overflowed with merriment and holiday visitors to celebrate.

John Vickers and his friend, Webb, gave a dinner to celebrate New Year's Eve. Lynda served as their hostess. Good champagne and lots of it. Everybody was lighthearted and gay. John Vickers in great form, his broken heart apparently completely forgotten.

Osmond, sitting opposite to Lynda, stretched out a long leg and played with her foot. Lynda's heart, brain and body soared to heaven in a sheet of white flame.

The dinner over. The band started. Osmond and Lynda waltzed half round the hall, but that was unwise for him.

For the remainder of the evening and until Auld Lang Syne reminded them of the New Year, they sat on the same sofa where their appreciation of Mozart had materialized.

They had fallen in love.

Lynda's traveling companion, John Vickers, had a date to meet his son on the Riviera, at Cap Martin. The son was coming out with his tutor.

Lynda wanted to remain in Switzerland, but John, essentially as her chaperone, would not hear of this. As an observer he considered their visit to Switzerland had taken an unfortunate turn of events, at least as far as Lynda was concerned. Lynda decided she had to go to the South of France.

Osmond felt gloomy about Lynda's impending trip to the South of France. As a result, he considered traveling there as well but he decided to stay in Switzerland. He had decided he should make a make a final, desperate, bid to improve his health. Perhaps, the beneficent sun would cure him; even work a miracle. He knew that nothing less than a miracle would be of any use.

"If only I had met you before this terrible disease" he said to Lynda.

It was ecstasy, after the grey gloom of winter in England and Switzerland, to wake up in that paradise of luxury, the sunny South of France. After the freezing whiteness of Swiss mornings, before the sun rises so belatedly, the ecstasy is even more pronounced.

"Gosh! This is heaven," thought Lynda, waking up her first morning.

Her room flooded with sunshine, the sea glittering. Little waves splashing lazily against the rocks. Mimosa orange trees and the fragrance of flowers was everywhere. The rich tenor of an Italian voice singing a serenade to the accompaniment of a mandolin on the terrace below was beautiful.

A knock at the door and the waiter brought in the perfect breakfast: rolls, croissants, coffee, butter and cherry jam. The weeks passed, everything pleasant and entertaining.

Everyday brought another letter from Osmond. He wrote he was curing well and would return to England in the Spring.

Lynda had a short run of luck at Blackjack and made fifty Louis on the outlay of one. Unfortunately, on subsequent nights, she lost it all.

The only snag about gambling is that tables would not return your money!

Return to England
1904, Aged 25

At last Spring had come, or, rather, early Summer, because it was the end of May. Lynda was on her way to Folkestone where Osmond had arrived the previous night. They had not seen each other since the winter when they fell in love.

It is incredible the heavy weather that was made in those days of any matter of personal sexual interest. It wasn't your own affair, but the concern of everyone else's curiosity.

There was the sharp dividing line between virtue and vice. Motor cars and telephones had not come into their own and made thereby the course of true love so incredibly difficult. Telephones were the monopoly of the financiers. The price of a Rolls or other reliable car was prohibitive. An inexpensive car was a hazard and never arrived at its destination. True love could never blossom.

In addition to these drawbacks there was the insistence and inconvenience of a chaperon. In line with the conventions, Lynda asked Griselda, a married friend, to accompany her to Folkestone.

The married friend had consented on the condition she could bring her golf clubs. She felt that two days of golf would revitalize her from the serfdom of domesticity.

Everything was consequently arranged, and Lynda engaged a bedroom and sitting room at a small hotel recommended by Griselda.

On this morning, however, things had gone wrong at Griselda's home. She could not, under any circumstances, leave until the following morning.

Lynda went to Folkestone alone. Osmond met her at the station. They got into a ramshackle open cab drawn by a broken-down old horse and drove to the rooms Griselda had recommended and left their luggage. It was lunch time and they went to Osmond's hotel. The place appeared very empty.

Osmond had taken a rather lavish bed-sitting room on the first floor. It faced south, the sun streamed in. For that afternoon, at least, the frustrations of convention, and chaperoning, were defeated.

But everything was hopelessly out of proportion. During dinner that night they discussed their immediate frustrations. Lynda had to remain at the Folkestone for at least two days. Griselda was arriving with her golf clubs the next morning. Osmond had to return to his English home the next day.

He told Lynda that marriage was impossible.

He had not given up hope of a cure, but he continued to lose weight. Tuberculosis was contagious and the deadliest affliction. If one had it, one was really an outcast and had no right to risk social relationships. If they married, Lynda would have to live in a Sanatorium.

"No," he concluded, "marriage would be a sin. So, let's wait."

Anyway, he would cure for another year and then see what happened.

Lynda thought it wouldn't help him much if she lived in the sanatorium. There was always the echo in her mind because of her father's illnesses.

In their discussions, Osmond had spoken about the perfection of his past experiences. Lynda suspected he meant other women. But he would not confide in her. Lynda believed that was because of his philosophy that being that silence is wisdom and that it was impossible to speak the Truth to women.

Lynda quoted Maeterlinck: "Love contains no complete and lasting happiness, save in the transparent atmosphere of perfect sincerity."

"You will have to tell me the Truth always, Osmond, promise me."

"Well, if we married, perhaps I would," he replied. "We are both jealous and you are hopelessly impulsive." He added grimly, "Truth never helps, it makes things worse!"

The next morning, he started on his journey back to Somerset.

Lynda became bored and disconsolate. She was left to play golf on the most exhausting up and down-hill course.

1904 was a perfect summer but most things worked out the wrong way. Love needs a background of tranquility and this is impossible to attain when surrounded by relations and well-meaning friends. Love needs a partner.

Lynda and her brother shared a house at Westward Ho! on the North Devon coast. This year, towards the end of June, Bino brought two friends down from Cambridge.

Osmond joined them all; together at last! The weeks in Westward Ho! seemed gold-dusted, the smell of lilac and gorse, the continuous glitter of sunshine on blue sea and yellow sands.

Lynda took a daily swim off the rocks in front of the house and Osmond, watching her, thought bitterly that love was a lesser value than health. Health meant life! His past had been a hopeless waste without his soul-mate.

There was a ledge on the side of the cliff below the garden; here, with books, rugs and atmosphere of sea pinks and ozone, Osmond spent most of the day.

He was reading Elizabeth Robbins, who had written "Health of the Body." Health, both mental and moral, should be the natural state. Good health enables a perfect society.

"Hell's Bells, where does that place me?" thought Osmond.

At the end of July Osmond returned to Somerset and Lynda to London. Her sister Priscilla expected her baby in August. As she was in good health there seemed little excuse for what followed.

The doctor, probably from some personal peculiarity, decided that Nature did not know her business and that he would improve and hasten her delivery of little Hugh, later known as Puck.

As a result, there were three weeks of critical illness for Priscilla. Nature, however, is forgiving, and in this case the baby arrived safely and in good health and Priscilla, miraculously, recovered.

Lynda, completely shattered by sleepless nights and anxiety for her sister, found herself physically defeated. She went to a friend's house in the Isle of Wight for a week's rest.

Osmond failed to understand. He wrote complaining that she had not written. He was returning to Switzerland. The only chance to meet would be at Dover where he would stay one night before departure.

Lynda went to Dover immediately, accompanied by a chaperone. The visit turned into a comedy of errors.

MINOR KEY: PART 3

Taking Osmond's Swiss Cure Seriously 1904, Aged 25

Taking the cure seriously meant leaving the comfortable hotel and going to a sanatorium, which was generally considered the best in Switzerland. It had been built and equipped sumptuously. Two thirds up the mountainside, it was reached by funicular railway. It stood on a plateau facing South. A lavish sun-trap. Sheltered from all winds by forests of pine trees, German money had built it and German genius was responsible for the perfection of its completion. A very great German doctor was in control of its management and organization.

Osmond liked the atmosphere. The people were interesting, and Dr. Thurman became a good friend. He laid out on his well sheltered sun-saturated balcony and cured and cured. He wrote music.

He wrote to Lynda – who had elected to go elsewhere with her elder brother for three months.

"She can't care much" he thought. "All that distance and I might die anytime" but Lynda really cared very much.

She felt miserable and loathed the consciousness of the long distance from Europe and was thankful when she landed in England again a few days before Christmas.

She had intended to go straight out to Switzerland and but alas! the complexities of life and one's duties!

Gloria (aka sister Priscilla) was seriously ill. Years before she'd had rheumatic fever and her heart had been affected, and the complications of her confinement that summer had apparently brought the trouble back.

The doctors insisted that sunshine, a dry atmosphere and complete rest were essential. Her husband could not leave his work and, consequently, everything devolved on Lynda.

Before the end of January, Lynda and Gloria with her hospital nurse were established in a luxurious suite in a hotel high up on the hill side above Cannes, and, as usual, the sun glittered down on the yellow and gold of oranges and Mimosa. Fragrance of flowers everywhere. Gloria lay on her bed or on the balcony most of the time in a blaze of sunshine, and at the end of March was very much better.

It was dull for Lynda who, finding the hotel increasingly expensive, thought she would make money at the tables. She made a weekly pilgrimage to Monte Carlo and only desisted after she had lost the best part of a hundred pounds.

Osmond's letters were satisfactory. He seemed very much contented and wrote that no place could give a better chance for a cure.

Osmond was finding life less dull than usual. Christmas time brought a Russian girl to the Sanatorium. She was not seriously ill, but had been ordered to rest from concert tours and performances.

She was a first-rate musician, temperament and technique, and although practice and work were verboten, she occasionally played on the well renown Bechstein piano in the music room. She played Rachmaninoff, Tchaikovsky and Brahms. Osmond listened transported to heaven.

This was fine, and the girl was attractive. Perfect figure, masses of brown curly hair hanging in a plait down to her waist, sensuous green eyes, very red lips and magnolia skin; and then as if this was not enough glamour, an English mother arrived with two perfectly beautiful daughters.

They were friends of Dr. Thurman and wanted recuperative rest, also the eldest girl had a friend curing, an Italian, whose career had been cut tragically short by hemorrhage.

"We had great times in Florence" he explained to Osmond, "and we would have been married but for this. The Sinclair's had rooms in that part of the Sanatorium known as Doctor's House. No tuberculosis patients were given these rooms. Cynthia and Celia were good skiers and having friends in Davos they occasionally went for all day expeditions.

At other times, when the elder sister paired off with the Italian, Celia frequently joined Osmond.

Celia was very lovely, the perfect illustration for "Gentlemen Prefer Blonds," and she had complete confidence in the attraction of her beauty.

Her mother called her a spoiled child and explained that she always insisted on having her own way.

Celia would join Osmond on his morning walk through the pine woods, link her arm in his, or slip her hand confidingly into his.

"Am I holding her hand or is she holding mine?" Osmond would ask himself and sitting in the sun-drenched shelter.

"Darling" she would say, "do you love me?"

One morning she asked: "What do you think of me, darling, really?"

"I think you are perfectly lovely," answered Osmond candidly,

"Your face is like a Greuze, even more beautiful."

"Darling, you are sweet. I'll give you my photograph and then you can see me all the time."

The next day she went down to Davos and bought a frame.

Green leather, one of the intimate types of frame, and so there it was, on his dressing table, Celia's eyes, beautiful and expressive, looking at him, reminding him of her all the time.

She went with him to the music room and listened to the Russian Zina, but neither Rachmaninoff nor Brahms meant anything to her, and she was inclined to whisper and laugh softly at her own remarks. This procedure was, of course, maddening to Osmond.

"These English girls" said Zina, "they understand nothing. Cold, like fish." Osmond hoped she was right.

Every night the routine was the same. One of them turned off the heat and threw open the long French windows. The snow and ice scudded in and fell in a little heap on the floor. They paused fractionally to consider the awesome mystery of stars and moon and stark cold everywhere.

And then hurrying into bed put out the light. It was impossible to think in that temperature and one prayed for sleep.

One night, towards the middle of March, when his room had iced down to zero and below, Osmond, in the satisfactory warmth of plentiful blankets and hot-water bottle, was suddenly wide awake. His door had opened and shut, and the key had turned in the lock.

"Heaven help me," thought Osmond, "the Russian!"

And there in the moonlight, stood Zina, looking like a fragile butterfly. Icy blasts stirred her inadequate and flimsy garments, her teeth chattering, and Osmond understood her to say that it would be his responsibility if she caught pneumonia and died.

Zina left the Sanatorium at the end of the week – fortunately in good health. Osmond, unnerved, completed the night's routine by locking his door. Nocturnal visits were not part of the cure.

MINOR KEY: PART 4

Two Timed at the Sanatorium
1905, Aged 26

The beginning of April, Lynda was coming to Davos.

Osmond had done his best to postpone her visit. Said everything was thawing and Davos was impossible. However, it had been impossible to put Lynda off.

She wanted to explain how mean she felt going away, and that Spring in Switzerland could be divine. Also, she was suffering economic stress and Paris was expensive. So, she duly arrived, and, although she did not know this, everything became very difficult for Osmond.

He met her at the top of the funicular. Lynda thought he looked much the same, perhaps a little thinner.

They went to lunch and Lynda, sitting with her back to the window, did not see Mrs. Sinclair, Celia and Cynthia lunching at a table in a sunny alcove. She was as usual very amusing and, despite the horror of the situation in which he found himself, they were both exhilarated by laughter.

After lunch they went up to his room and time passed in a flash. Sex dormant, the beatitude was being together.

Lynda forgot all the things she had planned to say, and the afternoon ended. As an afterthought, and to adhere to the conventions, Lynda said she would visit a friend who was also curing at the Sanatorium, a Mrs. Adams, an elderly woman who had been a neighbor in London.

Her room was on the first floor and in the same corridor as Osmond's. Lynda found him having tea, saturated in luxury – Persian rugs, armchairs, masses of hot-house flowers, piles of books, and a fire of logs in addition to central heating. Lynda did not stay long; the sun had gone down and the evening was gloomy. She said she would come again the next day.

Outside it was frightfully cold. She collected the sleigh she had brought with her. Starting warily, gradually gaining speed, faster and faster down the narrow zig-zag path, through the white silence of the pine woods, not a living creature about, a fraction of time and was back on the main street.

Osmond, at a later hour feeling uncertain, went down to face the music which he hoped would be pianissimo. In the hall he found Celia and Cynthia, and various men friends. They seemed in hilarious form.

"Osmond," they queried, "Who's the girl-friend?"

"Yes, darling, who is the creature?" asked Celia.

Osmond lost his head. Somehow dignity did not suit the occasion. "My cousin" he began. Someone interrupted, "Sure she's not your sister?" "No, my cousin," he repeated, "my father asked her to come and see me and report to him at home."

Now, as Osmond's father was a bishop, he expected this information would have a good effect, and it had. One does not cavil with the morals of a bishop.

"You must introduce me when next she comes up" said Celia.

"She's not coming," replied Osmond, "She's leaving for England, I think tomorrow."

"That's torn it," he thought. The difficulties now seemed overwhelming. Somehow, he must get a letter down to Lynda, and he must obtain unprejudiced advice.

After dinner he went to the Doctor's room. Dr. Thurman was smoking his after-dinner cigar. He made Osmond take an armchair and gave him a glass of port.

"So," He interrogated, "in trouble"? News of Lynda's visit had already percolated through to him.

Thurman was a great doctor and, also, one of the world's very few great men. He stood for Truth and the interests of humanity. He liked Osmond and recognized a touch of genius in the songs he had written. So much poetry and music, he thought, indicates genius.

Osmond had no problem explaining the situation to Dr. Thurman. He understood. Celia was devastatingly pretty; quite obviously Osmond had let her think he returned her warmhearted and artless affection.

The doctor said, "It's flattering to have the attentions of so pretty a girl." Osmond admitted this. "But Lynda is different," he said, "If I were not so ill, we should have been married."

The doctor made no comment. In his opinion marriage for consumptives was taboo. There was a silence for a moment and then the doctor said, "This Lynda, is she robust, and of what age?"

"A year younger than myself and absolutely robust, physically, mentally, morally and financially." Osmond smiled, the description of Lynda seemed apt and complete.

"Well," said the doctor, "she should marry and have children.

She is getting old; it is best to have children when one is young."

Osmond raised himself from the depths of the armchair. He felt the time had come for a final decision. "Her doctor," he asked,

"Tell me, exactly what is my chance of a cure?"

The doctor looked up at the long figure standing before him. The all-pervading gauntness, the think face, anxious eyes, sensual lips. He knew the exact state of Osmond's lungs – the ravage of the disease. He might live a few months, but a couple of years would be the extreme limit of possible time.

The doctor said, "Not marriage, Osmond, that would be a crime. Your best chance is to stay here through the summer months. Forget these silly women. You will come with me to Munich. We shall hear music."

Osmond smiled. That was the future, and there were present urgencies.

He explained that, somehow, he must get a note down to Lynda and prevent her coming up to the Sanatorium the next morning.

"That is wise," agreed the doctor. "There is talk. It would be a mistake for her to come again." He told Osmond to write the letter and he would guarantee she should have it by 10 am.

"It's getting late," he said, "you had better write it now, at my desk."

"Possibly," replied Osmond, but in his heart, he knew that Lynda and life were the same thing and that, without Lynda, nothing had been worthwhile.

On her breakfast tray the next morning Lynda found the letter. He wrote: "you must leave Davos at once. Under no circumstances must you come up to the Sanatorium again. If you did, it would mean I would have to leave. You must understand I cannot explain everything."

Actually, he explained nothing. To Lynda it was incomprehensible. She wrote him agonized entreaties, why could he not come down and see her? No telephones! Everything delayed action. Anyway, she had nowhere to go. It was needless extravagance to pay two hotel bills and her room was booked for a week, also, she anticipated, that this inexplicable frustration could not endure, that some alleviation must occur before the week ended.

Nothing, however, did occur. Osmond, apparently furious that she remained in Davos ceased to write. Each day, hour, minute dragged out its hopeless length. She dissolved into tears. She cried so much that the swollen condition of her eyes and face made it obligatory to stay in her room.

Lynda lived on black coffee, smoked innumerable cigarettes, and this orgy of coffee added to her inability to sleep. Outside, it seemed to snow ceaselessly. However, the dreadful week came to an end at last and Lynda did her best with her dilapidated appearance to make herself normal for the journey home.

A fellow traveler in her compartment was an Englishman, Vernon. Later in the evening they had dinner together, and it transpired he had spent the winter at the Sanatorium and knew Osmond. The dinner was good, the wine excellent and, the Grand Marnier, a golden sedative.

Also, Vernon spoke of Osmond. "Pour chap," he said, "he's very ill, but he has luck in some ways. Up there we called him 'Don Juan'."

"Don Juan!" echoed Lynda nervously. "Why?"

"Well, women like him. Two of them nearly came to scraps about him this winter."

"Who were they?"

"Oh, Zina and Celia. Celia, the Russian girl left. She really didn't count, but Celia – well, Celia is irresistible, and Osmond is devoted. I've got photographs of them in my case, I'll show them to you."

Back in the compartment, Vernon produced the photographs. He was an expert in photography, and he had wonderful effects of snow and ice. Switzerland in winter. Then there were the local ones of the Sanatorium and its inmates. Several of Osmond with Celia looking gay and very complete together.

Lynda's rage rose until she was nearly suffocated by the twin senses of indignation and jealousy.

All the misery of the past week and Osmond, as the photographs clearly showed, perfectly happy without her.

Celia was lovely. She, herself, had been unwanted. The mystery was explained. Worry, grief, disappointment, had all been wasted emotion. Lynda's philosophy was direct, she had no use for tact or subterfuge.

Now she explained: "I thought I was engaged to Osmond and came to Davos to see him."

"Oh, you were the girl who came to the Sanatorium. I was out that day, but it seems the facility management tried to avoid a scandal."

"Yes," said Lynda, "and I'm thankful you showed me exactly where I get off," and she laughed bitterly.

Vernon looked at her reflectively. Lynda was pretty, and had something quite magical, vital and attractive about her. "You have personality" he guessed, and added, "Osmond has had a run of luck, anyway."

Seething with the emotion that the photos had aroused, and in a white heat of jealousy Lynda wrote her letter to Osmond that night.

She said that he ought to have told her the Truth about Celia, and that if she had known she would not have come to Davos; that he had not given her a fair chance and that actually there was nothing more to be said.

She posted the letter in Paris. Osmond did not write back.

Weeks and months passed and there was no answer to her letter.

MINOR KEY: PART 5

Celia Raises Her Head, Again!
1905, Aged 26

Lynda made a determined effort. She would waste no more time on emotion. Most hotels were noisy. She had spent a week in Paris on her way home and had been totally unable to sleep owing to the continuous noise of traffic on a paved surface.

In London she took a room at Claridge's Hotel. It was no more expensive than other hotels and much quieter. In those prewar days, London beneficent in the spring.

One could almost revise Browning: "Oh to be in London, now that April is here." Piccadilly indeed seemed the hub of the Universe, and in spite of Empire building and the South African War the tragic elimination of the male population of Britain had not become acute.

The Season in full swing, the grey old houses looking gay with window boxes of geraniums, genister and marguerites.

Everyone bent on entertaining and being entertained.

Everywhere, one met one's friends, dances, theater parties, dinners, the Opera, Parsifal, The Ring perfect values for human appreciation. And now had come the wonderful addition to speed and progress, motor cars.

A friend had a Lanchester and often that summer they drove to Portsmouth garaged the car, and went by steamer over to the Isle of White.

Tennis, swimming, dancing and sailing, swiftly the days passed and at night sleep was profound.

One day the following winter a letter came from Osmond, he said he was sending her a waltz he had written. It arrived by the next post from his publishers. It was a gay little waltz, bright and trivial, and was dedicated to "Celia."

"Damn" said Lynda, "what can he think I'm made of?"

She wrote to Osmond, however, and told him she thought the song was good. At the end of the next week from the same publishers came a song dedicated to her.

It was called "The Heart that Knows"; which heart thought Lynda and concluded things were too subtle for her comprehension.

She wrote and thanked him and told him, which was true, that friends were urging her to go to St. Moritz the following month.

She had not made up her mind, but would he like to see her? "In any case" she added, "my interest towards you would be entirely maternal."

Osmond wrote by return asking her to come out and she went. She had been at St. Moritz for ten days and was dressing for dinner one night when her maid brought in a telegram which read "If you want to see me, come at once, I am having a hemorrhage. Love, Osmond."

All values collapsed; all time seemed wasted.

The only possible midnight route was located. It entailed a long sleigh drive over the mountains.

Minna, her maid, took charge and became very efficient. She packed a suitcase, had dinner sent up and forced Lynda to take some nourishment. She saw Lynda into the sleigh and packed her up warmly in rugs.

Lynda appeared shattered and inarticulate. She told her that a friend wag dying at Davos. He had a hemorrhage.

Minna was Swiss. She had gone to England and offered her services as ladies' maid being anxious to learn English. Conscientious therefore, and from an educational urge she read Lynda's letters whenever the opportunity occurred.

"That must be Osmond Wynne" she concluded "he lived in a Sanatorium at Davos."

This evening Minna dealt with the disorder in Lynda's room and thought it would be pleasant to have complete freedom for a little while.

She had a friend, a valet, staying at a neighboring hotel. She would spend the following evening with him.

Arriving at the bottom of the funicular, disheveled and sleepless Lynda met a friend, Muriel Talbot, all complete in skiing outfit. It was too early for the appearance of the sun and the morning was misty and frigidly cold.

Lynda explained why she had come and, Muriel anxious to help, said she would engage a room for her at the Hotel.

Lynda had done the last part of the journey by sleigh, the train she had connected did not go down to the Davos valley.

She paid the sleigh driver, left her suitcase with the porter and went up the funicular to the Sanatorium.

She asked to see Dr. Thurman and was shown to his room. The doctor said "He is better. Osmond told me to expect you."

"Thank God" said Lynda, and the agony of tension relaxed.

The doctor indicated an armchair and rang the bell "You must have coffee. You have traveled through the night and not slept. Is that not so?"

The coffee was soon brought. Lynda drank it and felt better.

"You will stay in Davos?" the doctor asked.

"Yes, I want to."

"Osmond must be kept quiet. No worry. This time he will recover."

"I understand and, Doctor, when I came up last year there was a misunderstanding. Will it be alright now?"

"Most certainly it will he alright I think it is good for him to see you, but today stay only for one hour, he's so tired, and it is not good that he should talk."

"I promise he will not talk, but Dr. Thurman, can he get better?"

The doctor felt that Lynda was a direct person like himself.

"No" he answered, "he cannot be cured. It is impossible."

"No chance?" asked Lynda.

"No," replied the doctor. "You know his room. It is the same as last year."

Lynda knocked lightly. With her hand on the door, she paused: one moment, and she would be with Osmond; a sensing of beatitude.

Osmond skin was tanned and freckled. He gave a misleading impression of health. His voice was very weak and husky and hollow.

Lynda would not let him talk. She told him that she had promised Dr. Thurman that she would not let him speak one word.

She sat beside his bed; his hand covered hers. All contacts between them seemed reestablished. They were encompassed and sedated by peace of their perfect understanding.

Lynda timed her visit and the hour ended. She went to the dressing table at the end of the room to fix her hat and there, in its sumptuous green frame, looking perfectly lovely, was Celia's photograph. No other photographs in the room.

"Hell!" thought Lynda, but she made no comment.

Absolute quiet the doctor had ordered, "no agitation, no worry."

The explanation must be postponed.

Next afternoon she came to see Osmond at about teatime. First, she met Dr. Thurman in the hall, and he reported Osmond to be much better.

"You can stay a little longer, perhaps two hours," he said

They had tea together. Later the curtains were drawn, the windows shut, and the lights put out.

An attendant knocked at the door and brought in a letter. He said there was to be an answer and he should wait outside.

Osmond having read, the letter groaned. "This is incredible" he murmured and then said to Lynda, "Celia is here. She was at St. Moritz and heard I was ill."

Lynda thought quickly. The paramount importance was that Osmond be kept quiet and calm.

No worry, no agitation, A meeting between herself and Celia must be avoided at all costs.

Lynda said, "Of course you must see her if she has come all that way. But Osmond I want to understand. Show me that letter." Lynda held her hand out for it, but Osmond held it high above his head. he said, "You will not see it."

"Darling, you said you did not care for her" pouted Lynda.

"I know, I know" said Osmond, "but that is all I did say." He looked both expectant and elated.

Lynda had to leave it at that. She met no one on her way out of the sanatorium and supposed Celia must be with the doctor.

The next morning, she got a note from Osmond. It said, "Come up this afternoon as usual and I will explain everything."

He explained nothing, and he never did. He said Celia's visit was lamentable, and her mother would be furious that she had gone back at once; that he had only seen her for five minutes.

"I did not know that they were at St. Moritz, and you, Lynda, are really to blame for the whole thing. Your maid had a friend at their hotel, and he spread the rumor I was dying."

There was the frustration one could not fight for Truth with the most charming man in the world who had had a hemorrhage and must be kept quiet, absolutely quiet, no worry, no agitation.

So, the tranquility of peace resettled between them and Lynda considered how to condense the questions she must ask before she left.

Anyway, she would leave it to the very last moment.

Each day he was getting a little stronger. Her luggage remained at St. Moritz. She had been at Davos nearly three weeks.

Suddenly Lynda felt the dismal incident of a cold coming on.

In the funicular one afternoon, she suddenly felt that indefinable sensation of a microbe invasion. There was a considerable amount of influenza in Davos.

She hurried through his room and onto the balcony.

"Osmond," she said, "I feel I'm getting a cold. I must go straight to St. Moritz where my luggage is stored."

"Catastrophic," murmured Osmond, "probably 'flu." A cold, he knew, would be fatal to him after his hemorrhage.

Lynda, scarcely breathing, hurried through the room and out of the door. She did not pause to say good-bye, Osmond must not risk infection.

Fortunately, she did not get flu, but all the things Lynda had planned to leave to the last moment to say were left unsaid.

As things happened, they never met again.

Lynda's temperature soared that night and the next two days she spent in bed. The third morning her temperature was down, and this was the date she had arranged to return to St. Moritz.

Muriel Talbot was going over with a British team entered for the Bob races.

Muriel came to her room bright and early and she and Lynda agreed that she was well enough to travel.

No one minded infection, everyone seemed to have flu at the moment, so Lynda got up and joined the combined operations of sleigh and train and, arriving duly at St. Moritz, went to bed feeling definitely the worse for wear.

The thermometer showed her temperature to be round about one hundred.

The next morning, very early, there was a knock on her door.

Muriel and a male friend came in. How did she feel; was she better they asked anxiously. Lynda was too sleepy to know how she felt, but they insisted that her temperature be taken, and it showed round 99.

"Definitely better," they said. "So what?" Lynda said and then they told her the horror of the happenings.

One of the members of the Davos team was a casualty with influenza. There was no one else from Davos in St. Moritz.

The British team would be disqualified from the bob sleigh races unless she, Lynda would fill the gap.

Lynda was too weak for opposition. She found herself dressed and on the bob sleigh.

A crew of eight and this form of winter sport was outside her experience.

"All you do," they insisted, "is swerve as we do. Are you ready? GO!"

And they went, swish through the icy air, fantastic, exhilarating, mad speed, hurtling high up ice banks, flashing down the straight – twisting corners, and then it happened.

An enormous ice bank – they took it well, almost over the edge and then crash. They were buried in snow. Nobody hurt seriously. Horseshoe Corner they called it, the worst hazard on the track.

Lynda understood it would have to be done again. Fortunately, they had a second chance. Everyone was laughing and joking.

She felt she was functioning in a separate world and seemed to be moving in a grey mistiness, all very blank. They walked to the bottom of the run and then back up the hill to the starting point.

Again, they settled in the bob.

Again, the perfect exhilaration of limitless speed. Again, a crash at the same corner. This time everyone was crest-fallen.

Lynda struggled back to her hotel and fell on her bed in a coma of exhaustion.

She was quite seriously ill with bronchial catarrh and stayed in bed three weeks. Unfortunately, Minna had left. Complete freedom at St. Mortiz had undermined her staying powers.

Lynda found her trunks packed in good order, but failed to remember the one or two items which Minna had purloined. For months she wondered how she had managed to mislay a very lovely black lace shawl, but she had no clue.

Lynda had friends at the hotel, Florence Lee and her son, and both had had influenza.

They suggested convalescence in sunshine and warmth and, in due course, drove in sleighs down the treacherous Moloya Pass.

Gradually leaving the snow behind they dropped into the soft greens and browns of the valley.

At Chiavenna, the Italian Frontier Village, they stopped and had lunch at the hotel and later in the afternoon took a train to Varenna.

How pleasant, how very pleasing, thought Lynda, looking down from her bedroom window. The deep blue of the Italian lake and the little terraced garden packed with flowers. It was a very small hotel built on the very edge of the lake.

The only other English people staying in the hotel were Mrs. Sinclair and her eldest daughter, Cynthia. Curious, thought Lynda, almost reminiscent of Alec Vernon. Naturally, they had become friends and gone places together.

One morning Cynthia and Lynda were sitting in the garden listening to the lapping water of the lake and watching the lizards disporting in the sun.

"Isn't Osmond Wynne your cousin"? asked Cynthia.

"No," said Lynda, without reflection.

"But you are very like him, and when you came up to the Sanatorium last year, he said you were his cousin." "That was, I expect, because it was an unconventional visit."

There was a pause and then Lynda queried, "Is your sister, Celia? I was at Davos when she came over this winter."

"Yes. She behaved quite madly. Old Villiers, who is a friend of mother's, had a valet who heard from your maid that Osmond was dying.

We were at dinner that night and Villiers said, "You remember Osmond Wynne? Well, poor chap, he's dying, probably dead by now."

"It was a bombshell to Celia, actually she nearly passed out, and next morning we found she had gone."

Lynda felt jealously anxious and asked: "Where is she now?"

"Oh, back in England."

That sounded about right, but one never could tell when people, like the Sinclair's, had independence and money.

"I wish" she said, "you would tell me the whole story."

"It's an odd affair; I have never understood it really" replied Cynthia "Last winter, at the beginning, Osmond appeared not to like Celia. He seemed to avoid her, but Celia always gets her own way. After a while, they were always together. Then, in the summer, she made mother take her to Munich. Osmond was there with Dr. Thurman."

Lynda remembered that Osmond had written about Munich and Wagner's music, he had written "Munich was all a glimpse of heaven to me."

Lynda's faith in herself shattered.

Cynthia asked: "Were you engaged to him?"

"I thought I was, more or less."

The next day the Sinclairs left for England.

Jealousy is a blinding force and wisdom has little chance against it.

Although Lynda and Osmond had not talked of the future, Lynda had planned to go back to Davos before the end of the month.

Now, with loss of self-confidence, her world was out of perspective, all the misery of doubt and suspicion brought to a head again.

She decided that she must get some assurance from Osmond, some help, and he must be told of her conversation with Cynthia. Lynda wrote the following to Osmond:

"The Sinclairs left today. I told Cynthia I was not your cousin and that last year when I came to see you, we were engaged. (Darling, you must forgive me, I thought we were.)

"It is vital now that you tell me about Celia, please don't leave things out."

I am in a torture of jealousy and uncertainty about you and me, Celia, all the time between us.

All Celia's letters that you won't show me.

Her photograph on your table. Loathsome creature. I hate her, but, darling, when all is said and done, only one thing matters really. It's what you want.

How you want things to be. Do you want to see me? To be with me?

Think before you write because I shall do as you want. Therefore, the only question, and be truthful for God's sake: is do you love me?"

When Lynda had mailed the letter, she felt much better about everything. She felt confident that Osmond would write and reassure her and that in a few days she would see him again in Davos.

She felt her letter was an S.O.S. and that he would understand and save her.

At lunch that day, my friend Godfrey Lee said, "Thank goodness, Lynda, you're in much better form today. Let's go on the lake this afternoon over to Bellagio."

Fate worked in just the opposite way.

Osmond was furious when he read Lynda's letter. What right had Lynda to discuss his affair with Celia with her sister, Cynthia.

And why make him out a liar over an extremely unimportant relationship?

Osmond was in a very bad temper, so he wrote two letters. The first to Celia.

"Darling, your sister met Lynda at Varenna, and they discussed me and you. When Lynda said she was engaged to me it was quite untrue and she knew it.

The Truth being that she had fixed in her own mind that I should cure through the years, during which time she would travel and see the world and when she returned, she would find me waiting for her, cured.

I am afraid that was all in her imagination. That's that, my Sweet, and this is only to thank you again for being so perfectly beautiful and for giving magical hours in grey days.

You convince men of Heaven on earth...the ultimate Truth. My love always, Osmond."

After writing this letter to Celia, Osmond took up his pen again and wrote grimly to Lynda.

"You ask for the Truth, well, it may be my illness, but I don't seem to care for you as much as I did. There is nothing to tell you. The doctor's report is not hopeful. My stepmother and sister are coming out at the end of the month to see me and I shall probably go back to England with them. Osmond."

Osmond read the letter to Lynda again. She wants the Truth so I will tell her, Osmond thought.

At this juncture, Osmond felt furious with Lynda, and anyway, Lynda's brother, Bino, had written asking him to give Lynda a push and to let her get on with her life; essentially telling Osmond to give her up. Bino said Lynda was making herself ill worrying about his illness. Bino wrote that it was about time Osmond stopped misleading people and that Osmond needed to make his settlement with life.

Lynda cried and thought that the sunshine was a compensation while Osmond waited with serenity for his final hemorrhage.

Lynda mused about her life striving and ending in nothing. Lynda could not help herself naively believing that Osmond would cure up to the very end.

The cynic that Osmond was, smirked.

MINOR KEY: PART 6

Husband to be Meyrick Enters the Picture 1906–1907, Aged 27–28

Lynda had taken a flat in London. In those days, bachelor flats were few and far between. However, this was a very small flat; bathroom, kitchen, sitting room and bedroom. It was in a large, uncompleted block. All the other flats untenanted. The place was frightening, especially when returning late at night. There were scores of open doors and empty spaces. She had a friend, a good companion, first class mind and a good sense of humour. He was a few years younger than herself.

Sometimes he stayed the night. A divan in the sitting room provided a spare bed.

Lynda concluded this was in order. His sleep over made her less nervous and it could do him no harm and might salvage him from the ubiquitous prostitute.

She heard from Osmond. He was in a Sanatorium in England. She wrote and told him she had acquired a flat and a boyfriend. "He has a good sense of humour and is years younger than me" she wrote.

Osmond replied: "Unwise I think, you are too jealous, impulsive and possessive."

Of course, Lynda knew it unwise. She had not intended the incident should be a lasting one, only through the winter months. Tennis and swimming were unsatisfactory.

To be alone meant thinking of Osmond continuously and what the hell was the good of that? He had turned her down! She had taken words as she always did at their face value.

However, conventional morality ruled in the social world and presently a drastic move was indicated. She let her flat and went to Cairo to join her brother in Egypt.

A mutual acquaintance, Dick Burton, felt a slight responsibility for Lynda's affairs.

Under pressure of secrecy Osmond had written to Burton the previous summer asking for news of Lynda and saying that owing to the force of circumstances he had given her up.

Dick had been staying with Lynda at a house her sister, Priscilla, had taken for the summer months on the Isle of Wight. It was spacious. A nursery wing contained her sister's baby and nurses, two nurses, no less.

The spare rooms were filled and there was an adequate domestic staff.

This meant that Lynda had gone back to looking after people; the responsibility is necessarily absorbing. As a result, Dick wrote in answer to Osmond's letter that Lynda was very well and happy. "Good" thought Osmond, "A very good thing." He felt virtuous.

Osmond thought that he had done the right thing to finally explicitly break up.

Osmond remembered that Doctor Thurman was always right. He had always said Lynda must marry and have children. "She is getting old,"

Lynda was 27 and Osmond was28. Much time had passed.

Osmond knew that Lynda was the completion of himself. The masculine and feminine component fractions that exist in men and women, should they meet, become complete harmony and entirety.

How often they must miss meeting, thought Osmond, but he considered that Lynda and himself were proof of Otto Weinger's theory.

"She is too direct," he reflected, "Nothing subtle about her, and her unfortunate passion for Truth is quite impractical."

Periodically Osmond received picture postcards of pyramids and tombs from Egypt; all from the civilizations of 6000 BC.

MINOR KEY: PART 7

Lynda Travels to Egypt, Osmond Dies 1906, Aged 27

It was the end of the Cairo season. Lynda had returned from a trip down the Nile, from the rose gardens of Aswan the ruins of Luxor and Karnak.

There was to be a dance at the hotel. Dick Burton came to dinner and brought a friend. The army had returned that day and now, after a month's maneuvers in the desert and after dinners of celebration; vital, virile full of enthusiasm, they poured into the ballroom.

Dick and Lynda rose to the occasion and partied with the best of the military officers.

When Lynda had first arrived in Cairo, Eric Lawson whom she had known through the years, had shown her round. They had done the bazaars, watched polo, played tennis and even attempted to climb the big pyramids. This endeavor had an ignominy.

Halfway up they had looked down with consequent paralysis, having neither of them a head for heights. The Arab guides provided salvation and, gesticulating and voluble like a crowd of monkeys, they had conveyed them back to base.

Tonight, she wondered if Eric would be at the dance. and then suddenly, there was a very positive twist.

"Save all your dances for me, Lynda," Eric said, and they were dancing perfect rhythm.

Afterwards they went out into the floodlit gardens. Chairs were placed by the palms on this sultry, tropical night.

A man can be an ecstasy, thought Lynda. Only the heart explains itself.

"That was wonderful, Lynda" exclaimed Eric, "Will you marry me?"

Lynda said vaguely "No, darling but thank you very much." She explained there was someone else.

That night at her dressing table Lynda looked with satisfaction at her reflected radiance and reconsidered her philosophy of love.

Obviously, there are different kinds of love, perhaps all equally soul gratifying.

She decided that she would go and see Osmond and ask him to forgive her for being so persistent and stupid.

In route from Egypt Lynda and her brother, Bino, stopped in Venice. They had come by Austrian Lloyd steamship from Alexandria.

Reading the English papers, there was news of Celia, leading with descriptions of her wedding. There were even some pictures.

Celia had married in London on April 9, 1906, two days earlier.

Lynda wondered what Osmond would feel about this.

The next morning the mail brought letters forwarded from England.

One from Osmond, written in his usual whimsical style. There was not a word about Celia.

Thank goodness, thank goodness, sang Lynda's heart. She felt optimistic. Maybe there was still a chance for me.

The winter was over anyway, and spring was arriving. She proceeded to open her other letters. One was a black edged envelope which she left to the last.

The writing was unfamiliar. She opened it carelessly. It was from Mrs. Wynne, Osmond's stepmother.

She wrote that Osmond had had a violent hemorrhage and died on April 4 two days after the date of his letter to Lynda.

"I know that this will be a great shock to you" wrote Mrs. Wynne. Lynda's heart registered the shock and she fainted. Dick Burton coming in from his adjoining room found her lying unconscious. He administered brandy and read the black edged letter.

He felt a qualm of conscience and wondered if he had behaved like a gentleman in Cairo.

Lynda thought: the Truth is deep in the heart's core and it is only the heart that knows the true meaning.

To Lynda, even in death, Osmond seemed a consistent presence.

He had died before Celia married just one week later, and before Lynda's return from Egypt.

Lynda wept, nights and days of tears until accumulation of events numbed remembrance.

For that short time when memory is acute, Osmond was with her: enigmatic, sardonic in his disastrous philosophy that "Truth never helps, it just makes things worse and worse."

Lynda remembered the poem by T. S. Elliot:

"Footfalls echo in the memory
Down the passage we did not take
Toward the door we never opened
Into the rose garden."

CHAPTER SIX

Seafield and the Death of Her Father
1904, Aged 25

T wo-thirds of my Fathers income came from Russia. About thirty years previously he and some friends, had invested considerable sums to develop one of the richest deposits of iron ore and coal in the Donetz Basin. In those days, it was called Usotka. It is now Stalino. Bino had gone out to Russia in the winter of 1903 for the consideration of a post in the company.

Life was very quiet at home, Priscilla was in France and my eldest brother was in Ireland. I had time for reading.

Father was prejudiced against novels – he called them pernicious poison – except Dickens, Zola, Thackeray and others of that ilk.

It is possibly true that when one is young and there is so much to learn, that fiction is a waste of time. I read chiefly philosophy:

Haeckel, Huxley, Schopenhauer, Laing, and did my best to probe the mysteries of life.

Anyway, I made my credo:

"The object of the world is life.
The objective of life is the world.
Man's objective is to be and do his best
Mentally, morally and physically.
For life's sake and the world's,
And in gratitude to God."

H.G. Wells currently was writing his most stimulating novels, although Ann Veronica and Togo Hunger came a few years later.

He wrote urging youth to be superlative in every way. One reflects what a waste it all was, two generations striving for perfection, striving and striving and ending in destruction beyond repair. In my opinion. Wells was unfair; he led us all up the garden path and then, when the wars came, he stood for victory.

I did my best to profit by his teaching. To be in healthy condition exercise was essential. I was lent ponies and cantered up and down Rotten Row in Hyde Park conscientiously three or four mornings each week. That winter there was an icy spell and all the lakes and rivers were frozen.

I was badly frustrated; Father was ill and I could not leave him. However, one night, after I had seen him comfortably settled in bed, a hansom cab was called, and I drove down to Ranelagh.

It was a wonderful night, great fires lit on the side of the lake. I met lots of friends and felt the virtue of exercise.

On Sunday afternoons, the Queen's Hall concerts, complete relaxation, sitting in a comparatively comfortable stall, eyes closed, one's senses carried on sound to the realm of the sublime.

That winter Father worried over his Russian investment which cousins had influenced him to put money into. It was going from bad to worse. More money was required to stave off disaster.

Although an ill man he still went to the city. One cold afternoon I was reading by the fire when the bell rang. Looking out I saw what was then known as a four-wheeler, the drabbest of vehicles always driven by veterans in palsied condition.

When I opened the front door, the driver indicated the interior of his cab. Inside my Father was lying semi-conscious. Sharp and I got him into the house and the doctor was sent for. He said my Father had been drugged.

When he recovered, he had no recollection of what had happened, but referred to a cheque about which he was mystified. A week or two later, the mystery was solved; he had signed a cheque for eight hundred pounds, of which he had no knowledge.

Shortly thereafter the Company went into liquidation. This business, I think, worried my Father to death for he believed in the company and in the integrity of his cousins, and he had influenced various friends to support them.

Suddenly at Seafield he had a chronic seizure. The poison flooded his brain and after a few days he died.

On the morning of the attack he had come very early to my room complaining of a terrible pain in his head. When the doctor came, he said he must remain in bed and keep quiet.

A cousin was returning to London that morning, she told me I was worrying unnecessarily. At dinner, the previous night, Father had drunk champagne saying that, he was doing this against Doctor's orders. This probably accounted for the pain in his head.

The curtains were drawn in father's room after lunch. I hoped that he would sleep. When I looked in two hours later, I found him fully dressed. The footman was putting on his shoes.

Unfortunately, Sharp was away for a few days, the footman said father had rung and insisted on getting up. We helped him downstairs, where he sat in a chair by the fire.

I was irritable that he had got up. I had been in the house all day. Outside the riot of spring, the sun was glistening on the sea. I gave Father his tea and, taciturn, went out for a short walk on the cliffs.

I had only gone a few yards when turning around I saw a maid hurrying toward me. On my return, I found Father standing by the tea table supported by footmen and the other maid. His face was flushed, and his eyes had lost their conscientiousness. We got him up to bed. The doctor arrived and telegrams were sent to Brinsley and Priscilla. He had died.

CHAPTER
SEVEN

Money Problems, Her Lover and
Meeting Her Husband, Meyrick
1905–1907, Aged 26–28

"There is no fun in playing in a world where everyone is cheating."

When one is young one is trusting and credulous. Father's will left his property to be divided equally between his four children. Previously in a marriage settlement 500 pounds per year was settled on each one of us; this income came from a perfectly safe investment in Barclays bank, one of the big four. The trustees were personal friends, one a director of the New Russia Company, and the other my father's solicitor. The racket started with maximum legal expenses for all communications, even the most unimportant thing being in quadruple.

We were asked to nominate a stockbroker, and, most unfortunately, gave the name of a cousin who was partner in a well-known firm. Before one had time for consideration all stocks were sold and replaced with unremunerative stock, chiefly English rails, and then I heard with dismay that the Bank shares had been sold. As these were gilt-edged there could have been no reason except the money to be earned on commission. But there it was.

Against our father's meticulous order and care we were up against it and playing a losing game. One thing leads to another. English rails were depressing, capital sliding downward and low interest rates. Argentine rails paid 7% interest, the Argentine was prosperous, and its future seemed secure. I transferred from British to Argentine rails. Today, one knows it was a mistake; except for debenture stock two thirds of the money invested in Argentine rails has been lost.

Then I made an even worse error. I persuaded my eldest brother to stay with some friends for the Hunt Ball. One of the men staying in the house had just returned from the Argentine. He had lived there for some years and gave glowing account of the country and its wealth. I advised my brother to take his financial advice, thinking that he might profitably reinvest two or three thousand. But what happened? The man was plausible. On his guarantees of a safe income (6% interest on gilt-edged stock) he put in a large sum and lost it all. That incident effected the whole course of his whole life and made it more difficult.

A few months after father's death Priscilla (also known as Glad) married; it had been a very quiet wedding. Mr. Ward plunged into suicidal depression, suggested that I should go abroad with him, and I persuaded a charming cousin to come with us. As usual, like a spoiled child, he insisted we should start the day after Priscilla's wedding. I had no time to leave things in order and this turned out to be even more frustrating than seemed possible at the time.

My visit abroad prolonged itself to six months, and when I returned Priscilla had moved furniture to her new house which included the complete contents of my bedroom, and although she generously offered me a home, my goods were scattered and I never collected them again. Very galling! I remember the shock when I found my denuded room.

Unfortunately, when we got to Paris the charming cousin and I succumbed to influenza and were supine for ten days. When we returned to consciousness, we found that Mr. Ward, instead of taking tickets to Vienna as previously agreed, had taken them for Davos which, he said he had done for my sake, as I should enjoy winter sports.

Bella and I were too weak to protest. He introduced us to George Moore who, as we wandered round the Louvre, told me the story of the lake. He volunteered to come to Davos, if Bella would give him consideration.

However, he remained in Paris and when we arrived in Davos, we found it too depressing, a miserable place, the hotel really a sanitarium. Bella hated it and arranged to return home after Christmas.

My eldest brother (this was before his financial disaster) came out, skied, played bridge, enjoyed himself and went back with Bella. Some cousins of mine were staying in the hotel and Mr. Ward and I joined up with them.

During these weeks I made friends with the most attractive man in the world, he had consumption, had it for years and was not getting better. He said he did not mind, he had had a wonderful time, it was well worth burning the candle at both ends.

"No regrets?" I queried. "No none" he said.

Eventually it was decided that he would cure assiduously and when he was better, we would be married. In the meantime, I was selfish. I had done so much nursing, looking after my father and Priscilla. I was influenced by wanderlust, also by the fact that Desmond was content with our experience. The realization of changed values is difficult when every normal value becomes valueless.

Dennis came to Seafield. Summer weeks were perfect, but there were frustrations of every kind. He had tuberculosis which was an insurmountable obstacle to marriage. So of course, things did not go according to plan.

I went to America for three months that fall. On my return, when I should have gone to Davos, I found Priscilla in a state of critical illness; her heart had been affected from a nerve racking pregnancy and confinement. The doctor had ordered a complete rest in the South of France.

Her husband, Lord Stalbridge, could not leave England, so I took her out there. At the end of the winter she was much better, and I went on to Davos. Those six months had been unfortunate. My friend, Dennis, had a volatile temperament and it seemed a case of "autre temps, autre amour." To what extent I never knew for there was too much misunderstanding and too little honesty.

But when one meets a person who is the completion of oneself, one never tunes in perfectly again. During the next two years we met only for a very short time but, even then, there was no explanation, no Truth. The doctor said he had no chance of recovery and, the next spring, he died. Always I had to remember the other girl's photograph was on his table.

Epitaph: Oh, sorrow left behind, to thee also farewell.

The full story of this unhappy, and secret, love affair is given in "Minor Key" which was probably written in June 1908.

May 5, 1906

I am going to give up keeping a diary and keep this book for composition of essays and short stories.

May 1906. Cleveland Gardens, Manchester Gate

I have been here for nearly three weeks. Have bought and sold a few securities. Hope for good results in getting out of English stocks into American rails. The arrogance of stockbrokers is somewhat confusing to the uninitiated.

I went to Wagner's Ring Cycle with Priscilla. Absolutely sublime. Wagner is among the finest philosophers. He makes one resigned to everything and the tears he draws are those from an exquisite agony.

July 26, 1906. Bembridge, Isle of Wight

Today I have personal ambition and it is my first. I should like to get hold of an original theme for a book.

November 21, 1906

Fergus goes to Egypt next week.

December 30, 1906

Another year finished and I can thank God for things as they are. It has been a good year although it is only in the past four months that I have felt personally contented. I really had almost forgotten how to feel happy.

January 23, 1907. Gina House Hotel, Pyramids, Egypt

Arrived yesterday in Egypt.

April 16, 1907

Fergus and Capt. Fitzgerald went to Trieste two days ago to fetch the motor which had been shipped from Alexandria. Mrs. Fitzgerald and I went to Padua to meet them. At Venice station we had a horrible time because we had two dogs and a hundred small boxes, etc.

The manager and staff mistook uniformed Capt. Fitzgerald for our chauffeur. They treated him accordingly with considerable bonhomie. He was extremely tired tonight. When the Italian porters jocularly asked him to lend them a hand and plied him with gentle bad language about his car. His simply lost his temper.

April 19, 1907

Padua contains two beautiful churches, but I confess, I am tired of churches, I think I overdid them in Venice.

April 22, 1907. Milan

We spent a day at Verona sightseeing. The Colosseum is in splendid condition. I think it would be a splendid monument of the present time to erect a Colosseum around Lords in place of its vulgar wooden sheds.

I saw the houses of Romeo and Juliet and many churches.

The Duomo contains Titan's "Assumption," which is perfect. The Virgin is the embodiment of sorrow and pity for a mistaken world.

We packed into the motor at 10 a.m. yesterday morning and had a splendid drive.

May 9, 1907. 42 Horton Court, London W.8

My flat is comfortable. It is possible to live on very little, in fact almost nothing. If only I can get something to do, some interesting and lucrative employment. One must justify one's existence. It is futile to exist if one wakes up in the morning feeling that the day ahead is not worth the effort it takes to face it. I suppose my compensation is that I have certainly enjoyed many things.

July 11, 1907

To be poor is demoralizing, not to pay one's bills is immoral. Consequently, I am having an irregular life. I am paying my bills and am exceedingly poor. This seems a contradiction, but the payment of bills is completely demoralizing.

I went to a varsity cricket match yesterday. Meyrick Payne did not play cricket as well as he could and should have done. However, Cambridge won by five wickets. He will possibly re-establish his reputation by playing for Middlesex.

Explanatory note by CMP. Although there is no proof, it seems likely that Charlotte married my grandfather in haste and on the rebound from her tragic affair described in Minor Key. As a frustrated and somewhat discontented wife, she and her girlfriend went looking for adventure in Europe. This adventure, if it is Charlotte's, is described in her story called "Kindred Soul", which follows in the next two chapters.

STORIES

KINDRED SOUL: PART 1

Two Wives, Alicia and Louise, Set off for Adventure 1903

Alicia Babington and Louise Devereux were great friends, they were the same type of woman, congenial to each other.

There were many points on which they could mutually sympathize. The one most accentuated and in the foreground of their highly strung minds was the absolute uncongenial temperaments of their respective husbands.

Both women had had short engagements and during that love-blinded period the true nature of their spouses, had curiously escaped them.

John's sullen temper, Frank's coarse candor had been buried in eloquent silences and misconstrued in misty glances.

Now, after some years of married life, they were under no delusions.

The awakening, however, had left its mark in a certain scared facial expression and a wasteful loss of self-confidence. This latter being caused by the constant repression of individuality necessary to make life bearable with Frank and John.

Both Alicia and Louise felt keenly this wrong inflicted on their personalities and this sorrow combined with continued self-repression had brought each to the verge of a shattered nervous system.

So out of gear were their constitutions that Doctor Todwell, a mutual medical adviser, pronounced that a complete change essential for both.

It was early spring, March, and the question was where to go.

Frank and John were reluctant to miss the last days of the hunting season and, as Todwell pointed out, a complete change meant severance of all domestic ties.

Finally, after much talk and indecision, the women decided on the Italian Lakes.

"There, anyway," said Todwell, on a respective visit to each of his patients, "you will find peace."

So, one morning the husbands, Frank and John, found themselves on the Victoria platform administering final words of advice to their wives.

It was a raw, cold morning. Both men had a tinge of mauve in their normally bronze complexions.

Louise and Alicia buried in furs, each wearing a large bunch of violets looked cozy, warm and singularly attractive.

"You must be very careful," said John, "with whom you associate. Louise has an unfortunate habit of talking to everybody."

"Well, Alicia won't allow that, you hate the casual acquaintance, don't you darling?"

"Yes," sighed Alicia, "and everybody bores me. I suppose I am an uncommon type and it's difficult to meet one's kindred souls."

"Kindred, fiddle-sticks," said Frank, "you are very ordinary, only somewhat eccentric."

This was too much for Alicia; "ordinary" was the most insulting epithet he could have chosen.

"Goodbye Frank" she said stiffly, giving him a slight peck.

"Goodbye Mr. Devereux," and she got into the train.

Louise followed her and after a few minutes of desultory conversation, the train started.

Frank and John waved goodbye, then the husbands linked arms and strolled nonchalantly down the platform.

"Hope they will have an amusing time," said Frank, "personally Italian Lakes do not appeal to me, nothing to do there but sit and look at mountains. However, as I said before, Alicia is so eccentric, she'll probably think that great fun."

"Yes," John assented, "Women have a strange idea of amusement. My dear fellow I can sympathize with you if you think Alicia is eccentric. Louise is absolutely mad." Frank started and looked at his friend with some anxiety.

"Say, old fellow, is it wise to let them go like this?"

John shrugged his shoulders. "Louise is harmless," he said reassuringly, warming to the subject "but, she is certainly mad. Her sense of humour is so extraordinary. The other day she opened a letter of mine, a letter she had no right to see, the whole thing caused a most unnecessary disturbance."

Frank smiled, "She does not sound so harmless, friend."

John saw no humour in the situation, the injury inflicted was of too recent a date, his indignation smoldered fiercely.

"Women" he said, "have no sense of right and wrong, their logic is hopeless."

"Louise, to prove herself right told me that two negatives make an affirmative. I call that flying off on a tangent. What could she have meant?"

"Of course, my dear fellow, in a woman's muddle-headed way, she meant that two wrongs make a right."

"Hah, hah," laughed John, "I had the whole situation upside down."

Still laughing, they hailed a hansom cab and they drove to their bachelors club.

KINDRED SOUL: PART 2

Meeting the Strange Mr. Frampton

Louise and Alicia had decided to break the journey. They stopped at Milan.

Whilst traveling they had made the acquaintance of a fellow traveler, Mr. Frampton. He was a remarkable looking man and had attracted their attention, even during the time of anguish and self-absorption on the Channel.

Impervious to rolling decks and the suffering of others, he had paced grimly backwards and forwards. An almost majestic figure. The sickly pallor of his complexion denoted a bilious tendency, but the square jaw set in grim determination showed, to the psychologist, a will of iron.

They arrived at Milan late at night and with maids, dressing cases, two rugs and other traveling essentials, got in the omnibus of the Hotel de Ville.

Then looming out of the darkness they saw Frampton's remarkable face at the window.

He was addressing the porter in fluent Italian and his tones were those of expostulation.

Suddenly, he changed into English. "Ladies," he said "apparently there is no room for me in this bus, but as my Doctor has told me on no account to risk night air, I must ask one of you to get out."

Louise deftly hurled her dressing case and smallest hold all onto the knees of her maid." "There's lots of room really" she said genially, and Frampton got in.

At the hotel, with consistent self-solicitude, he succeeded in complete annexation of the entire staff and was shown to his room, while Alicia and Louise waited in the hall.

The next day, on entering the Cathedral, they encountered him again. He said good morning and appeared to be guiltily conscious of his discourtesy the night before.

"The truth is I am such an invalid, a journey to me contains every species of risk. It is only with the greatest care and contrivance that I can bring myself safely from point to point. You understand I can give no thought to the trivial superficiality of manners."

Louise and Alicia, deeply sympathetic women, took his point of view, manners seemed at a discount.

"We are looking for a guide," said Louise.

"So am I" said Mr. Frampton, and his eyes alighting on an official-looking ruffian, he annexed him and suggested that they should go around together.

After the glare and bustle of the streets, the religious peace of the Cathedral was soothing to the jaded nerves of the two women. It seemed wholly delightful to be admiring saints and windows in dim subdued light in the company of Mr. Frampton.

This latter, however, kept up a ceaseless inter-locution with the guide and this being in Italian, Alicia and Louise did not further their knowledge.

On starting the ascent to the roof of the Cathedral, they were quickly left behind.

Mr. Frampton, despite the delicacy of his constitution, had followed the guide up the winding stairs with brisk alacrity. Finding themselves alone listening to the echo of fast receding footsteps, Alicia was very much annoyed.

"It is most insulting" she said "to leave us like this, without a guide, of course the man is a cad. I took his measure at first glance. So stupid of you Louise to consent to go around with him. You have no perception and no dignity."

Louise bore the outburst calmly. "I perceive you have lost your temper Alicia and are incapable of seeing things in their proper light. You should be thankful that Mr. Frampton's physical superiority prevented you from hopelessly overtaxing your strength."

Alicia was, however, thoroughly irate. Meeting Mr. Frampton that night in the hall of the hotel, she passed him with averted head.

It was therefore in a somewhat tentative manner that he came up to them later, when they were sitting down to dinner.

"What happened to you both this morning?" he inquired; his eyes fixed on Alicia who remained silent.

Louise explained "You were wise," said Mr. Frampton, "it was absurd of me to go up those stairs. I had a bad heart palpitation this afternoon."

Alicia looked up. Encountering faded violet eyes set in a grey, tired face, her own lost their hostility.

"Have you tried these?" she asked, fumbling in her bag purse and producing a small box. "I have fearful palpitations, but these Pennant pills invariably stop them."

Mr. Frampton took the box; he was full of gratitude.

"I shall see you later at La Scala Opera House" he said and moved back to his table. The Opera was The Queen of Spades.

Tchaikovsky's broken chords and minor themes so absorbed Alicia and Louise, it was not until the end of the second act they noticed Mr. Frampton sitting a few rows in front of them.

Among the somewhat squalid Italian audience, he looked his best, in fact beyond his best, his best being emphasized by contrast. Alicia and Louise felt a glow of patriotic pride.

"So, English," murmured Alicia, "but" looking at Louise with frightened eyes, "imagine Frank and John here."

"Frank and John," repeated Louise and, as the orchestra restarted with on a soul vibrating chord, she shivered. Frank and John with Tchaikovsky!

The idea was discordant. She exchanged a glance of heartfelt sympathy with Alicia, then both women let their eyes rest on Mr. Frampton, who was sitting absorbed and content.

After the opera he came up to them, his grey face had a slight tinge of colour and his eyes glowed.

"Glorious," he said, sinking into a vacant stall by Alicia. "It's vandalism to wait for the Ballet but this being Milan, of course we must."

Louise smiled and saw by Alicia's complete change of manner that she thought she had found a kindred soul.

Next morning Louise and Alicia started for Varenna.

Mr. Frampton had told them that Bellagio was his destination. They were surprised therefore that evening to see him enter the dining-room of their hotel.

Alicia coloured slightly as she encountered his penetrating gaze. He explained he had changed his plans, having heard that Varenna gets the sun two hours before the other side of the lake.

She formed an opinion which did not coincide with his statement. The Italian lakes are perfect. Blue sky, blue water, green mountains; for this to be typical the sun must beat down gloriously. The water must reflect the sun in a thousand shimmers, the mountain sides simmer in a breathless atmosphere and one must feel all exertion an effort.

Alicia had felt that in this perfect spot something was wanting.

"Heaven itself would be hopeless if one were in it alone."

She felt that a kindred soul was the necessary adjunct to an Italian Lake. Without, it became as Hamlet with the soliloquy omitted.

Louise was delightful but was too dogmatic to be the ideal companion.

When Mr. Frampton entered the dining room she felt her pulses quicken.

He looked so tired, jaded, he made her think of autumn leaves. His trim figure had a tired stoop. His hawk like, aristocratic face a blasé expression. His hair and complexion toned together in shades of grey and his eyes seemed faded from the glare of a well lived past.

She wondered, was he Hamlet!

The Hotel at Varenna is delightful. Its balconies and terraces overlook the lake and one's chief occupation is to join the lizards in the garden and disport oneself in the sunshine.

For people of greater energy there was a steamer that starts at all hours for all points of the lake.

Mr. Frampton was one of these. The first week he started off at early dawn and was only seen in the evening, when in a repellent manner, he buried himself in a newspaper.

Alicia was rather hurt at this, but nothing could dampen Louise's spirits. The air of the lakes seemed to have intoxicated her.

Louise's sense of humour was intensified, and she saw only the comic side of things. Her laugh rang out again and again. Louise rather prided herself on her laugh, she had been told it was infectious. It certainly reminded one of the gurgling of some effervescent liquid, when its cork is drawn. However, it jarred on Mr. Frampton.

Alicia, sitting opposite to him at dinner, saw him flinch and turn a greyer hue each time Louise laughed.

She told this to Louise, who with her intensified sense of humour, thought this so funny that the mere sight of Frampton made her smile.

One morning they were sitting in the garden, Alicia was expostulating: "It's perfectly evident your laugh has got on Mr. Frampton's nerves. Last night it was entirely your laugh that made him leave the dining room; he crumpled up his paper, looked murderous and went to bed."

"Preposterous Person!" said Louisa.

"To whom do you refer?" asked a hollow voice beside them, where stood Mr. Frampton.

He had come silently around the corner of the terrace. Alicia gasped.

Louisa went into peals of laughter. Mr. Frampton stood there; his look only equalled by the contempt in his tone as he asked Alicia if her friend was often subject to such distressing fits of hysteria.

Louise felt as if she had received a cold douche. However, she regained her composure.

"I have an intense sense of humour," she explained lamely.

"Humorists generally provide the jest, not the laughter," Mr. Frampton remarked acidly.

"Certainly," said Louisa, "you are the humorist."

Mr. Frampton smiled, a little ashamed of his peevish display of temper.

"My dear lady" he said, "that is the last thing I can be accused of. I see misery, misfortune, crime on all sides. I see pain and death. But I see no joke, no food for humour."

"What a pessimistic view. You see only the shadows!" Louisa responded.

"Yes, I see it, a grey world of shadows." Mr. Frampton continued.

"You think it is, but even that is a mistake. What you think you see is the fictitious effect of the rays of the sun. There is no colour in anything really. There is no Truth in anything. Everything is wrong."

"Tout est pour la meilleur, dans la meilleur des mondes," retorted Alicia.

"Nature is always right, but it is people like you, Mr. Frampton, who do not give her a chance."

"Chance? Chance?" echoed Mr. Frampton.

The word seemed to rouse him to a frenzy of excitement.

"Chance is its explanation, nature herself is chance. The solar system is chance. The fundamental origin of the essence of things is chance. Chance is the answer to the riddle; the Riddle of the Universe."

He was transported by his subject, his voice trembled, he was an enthusiast.

"Chance," he repeated, "is the answer; and chance explains everything. The muddle of the world. There is no order, no system, no reason for anything. The whole thing is blind, infinite chance. Isn't it simple? It explains everything I am writing about now. The world will know. Existence will be simplified. There will be an end of strenuous endeavor, futile strife. Everything will be substituted by a magnificent resignation to the vagaries of chance."

Louisa looked pensive. She felt that to have laughed at the man who had solved the Riddle of the Universe, was a faux pas she could hardly hope to live down.

It appeared that Mr. Frampton had given up his life to scientific research. From his amassed knowledge he had deducted a theory of the universe.

In his mind, this theory had been mathematically proved. His was the one mind on which the Truth had dawned and, as he explained to Louisa, when a thing is mathematically proven, there is no room for doubt.

He had solved the Riddle of the Universe.

Both women felt now that he was indeed one of the world's great men and listened with rapt attention to his words of wisdom.

Mr. Frampton was far from averse to a sympathetic audience and became friendly and sociable.

Three weeks passed pleasantly; perpetual sunshine, a calm lake, congenial companionship, even Frampton admitted that life was bearable.

One day they had gone down on the little hotel launch to the Bellagio. It was an ideal spot some distance from Varenna.

They had taken their picnic lunch with them and had it on the grass at the edge of the lake.

Afterwards they were enjoying the blissful siesta of the well-nourished, when suddenly Frampton aroused himself and looked at his watch.

"By Jove!" he said, "we must be moving. My friend McGregor arrives this afternoon. I am going to Rome with him tonight."

This was sad news. Alicia, with real sorrow in her eyes, expostulated: "Do you think you are wise, Mr. Frampton? You have been complaining of palpitations and you look far from well today."

Louise studied him. Alicia wag right. He looked old and haggard and there was an indescribable wild look in his eyes.

At Alicia's remark he laughed. The laugh matched his eyes. It rang wild and discordant. Some change had come over him, he was subtle, mysterious.

"I have work to do" he said, "and cannot loiter longer."

When they arrived back at Varenna, Louise went with Alicia to her room.

Alicia flung herself on the sofa wearily; she seemed rather bored of life. The windows were wide open, the sun poured in. The lake outside looked, as usual, calm, beautiful and blue.

"Louise," she said "I am tired of this place, it will be impossible when Mr. Frampton leaves."

"We shall miss him horribly" agreed Louise, "he has been such a guide, philosopher and friend."

"Such a genius! So Immensely simpatico!"

"So musical. Such a temperament!"

"Never again, Louise, shall I meet such kindred soul."

There were tears in Alicia's voice. Louise, standing in the sunshine at the window, felt the Frampton's departure.

He left the future grey and hopeless. His powerful personality had indeed completely absorbed their time and thought, even their letters to their husbands had shown the time with Frampton to be an all engrossing subject.

Frank had written that from Alicia's description, Mr. Frampton appeared to be an adventurer of the worst type. He advised her to drop so undesirable an acquaintance.

Alicia had laughed and said "Poor Frank! So, kind! So good! but so unutterably ...." She was too English even to think the missing word.

At six that evening, hearing the hotel bus come around, they went down to wish him good-bye. The bus was piled with luggage.

The manager was looking at his watch. The concierge was there. The usual crowd of domestics stood officiously around. But there was no sign of Mr. Frampton. A few minutes passed; the manager eyed his watch.

"He must be quick, or he will miss the train" he said.

At this minute a sound of scuffling was heard. All eyes turned towards it.

Apparently, Mr. Frampton had reconsidered his decision to leave Varenna. His friend, a strong red-headed Scot, named McGregor, was urging him forcibly not to be of such a vacillating nature.

Bang! Scuffle down the stairs they fell. Mr. Frampton had no chance with the strong Scot, even though he was doing his best, biting and kicking futilely.

Louise and Alicia rushed towards him. "What is the matter Mr. Frampton"? they asked. At the sound of their voices he became suddenly quiet, and shook himself free of the Scot.

"Everything is the matter" he said. "The whole world is turning upside down and McGregor won't let me stop to steady it."

"Come now," said McGregor, "do be sensible, you can do that just as well at the station."

"At the station, so I can" said Frampton, and dashing to the bus, he scrambled in. His friend followed him.

"Good–bye you Cochin China Chickens" he called to Louise and Alicia as he waved them farewell.

The manager touched his head knowingly.

"Poor gentleman" the manager said.

Louise stood dazed, even petrified.

But the collapse of Alicia with a heart palpitation called Louise to immediate action.

The manager helped her escort Alicia to her room. There they laid her on her sofa and, after a stiff dose of brandy and with the aid of smelling salts and other restoratives, she gradually became calm. Louise sat beside her thinking.

Later the maid brought in the evening post.

There was a letter from Frank. Alicia opened it languidly with an utter lack of interest but an exclamation suddenly broke from her.

"What is it Alicia?"

"My dear, it's about Mr. Frampton."

Louise shuddered.

"Listen to what Frank writes: I hope you heeded warning about Edward Frampton, I have heard all about him. He is a lunatic and has been in several asylums. He is generally harmless, but occasionally not so."

"The Johnsons know all about him. He generally travels with his keeper, a red-headed Scot. My one fear, knowing how eccentric you are, is that you may find in him a kindred soul."

Alicia stopped and savagely tore up her letter. Then, she laughed hysterically, perhaps at her own hot-headed nature.

They returned to England shortly. Both were curiously reticent about their trip to Varenna.

CHAPTER EIGHT

Charlotte's Secret Wedding and Birth of First Child 1907–1908, Aged 28

"To restore sanity sometimes a strong antidote is necessary" (like marriage and getting pregnant).

I had a friend at Cambridge, several years younger than myself, an excellent companion who had all the attributes: a good athlete, sense of humour, first class mind, musical talent and temperament, and although I never meant to marry him, he showed great determination and at a certain date, when he was due to go abroad, I found myself coming out of a registry office, married. Almost immediately Meyrick was posted to the Sudan.

November 16, 1907
(written after her secret marriage to Meyrick Payne)

I must try to unravel the muddle in this diary. Meyrick sees fit not to tell his employer and friends. Eventually, he wrote to say that he has told his people. I get a copy of his unopened letter forwarded from Seafield.

Calculating that his people must have heard two days past, I write and apologize to them for the indiscretion of marriage. However, they have not received a letter from him. Of course, my letter is a bombshell.

*Charlotte at the time
of her marriage*

Meyrick writes to his brother-in-law Bino to tell him. Bino's narrow prejudices are so upset that he talks to me with pursed lips and eyes of contempt, probably because I am already pregnant. This strained attitude of his reduces me to an extreme of flippancy.

June 1908

Restart of life. Baby was christened on Sunday, Iris Winifred. I have got a nurse who I do not yet thoroughly understand, but she impresses me with confidence.

I wrote a story ten days ago. (Probably Minor Key)

December 10, 1908

"Be ye therefore, perfect even as your Father in heaven is perfect."

Everybody is a mass of faults and imperfections. I know that I am hard, sordid and mean. If I wasn't, I should be soft, generous and extravagant and, owing to an insufficient income, should be in false position.

I know I should be much nicer and more affectionate to Meyrick, who writes me such nice letters and who I now find it so difficult to remember.

March 1909

Meyrick has returned from the Sudan. He arrived at the embarrassing hour of midnight. When one's husband is a total stranger this is not really the most tactful thing to do.

June 16, 1909

Meyrick went off to the Sudan again yesterday. I miss him very much especially this morning, as on returning to my peaceful cottage I find

Margaret and Nurse have had a row. Margaret while losing her temper accuses Nurse of everything horrible under the sun.

July 4, 1909

"Mon Dieu, Mon Dieu, Mon Dieu!"

I have started housekeeping at Seafield this morning. We arrived down – baby, Nurse and self – last Wednesday. On descending into kitchen this morning found same in congested condition... strewed largely with baby's nappies.

Husband Meyrick Whitmore Payne in his cricket garb.

This I admit upsets me, and quivering with disapproval, I take the dirty nappies upstairs and asked Lisa's nurse to have them washed elsewhere. Lisa is perfectly furious.

At lunch she understandably quits and tells me that she has only kept in with me for Bino's sake, that I have always rubbed her the wrong way, that I am impossible to live with and she intends to take the twins elsewhere for summer. She also adds that I have done nothing but insult her since I have been here, which is a most absolute lie.

I keep extremely calm under this avalanche of unfriendly feeling and am now wondering what will happen next. From a financial point of view, she will be an absolute ass if she smashes up the present baby party, which promises to run all right; if only, I get a kitchen maid to ease her personal feelings.

August 26, 1909

This plan has turned out a success despite vicissitudes innumerable. The twins look wonderfully stronger. I have given up tennis. Priscilla and Bino both have weak hearts, so golf is their only game.

The housekeeping has not succeeded to the ten shillings per head requirement, but Lisa will not eat fatty foods and as Priscilla gets in the family way, has longings for caviar, finally miscarries and has to be fed on chicken and sole, and as Puck cannot eat veal or beef and the babies have to have chicken broth etc., and Bino has to be dieted, chiefly on cream, one has to get a good deal for the money. The household averages sixteen heads and the books nine pounds ten shillings weekly.

Three years later I left my small daughter, Iris, then eighteen months old, with Priscilla, whose son was four years old, and who had a perfect nursery house and garden, and I went to the Sudan, certainly not God's own country. It seemed to me hell on earth.

My cabin on the ship was packed with cockroaches. The horror started in the Red Sea. I slept on deck but was forced to use the cabin for clothing purposes. In the mornings I could hear them scattering on my approach. Clink, clink, a cockroach stampede.

At Port Sudan, it was all flies and spiders and scorpions.

October 28, 1909. Red Sea Provinces, Sudan

A sultry spot. The heat is stupendous. My head is dizzy from it. My feet swollen. I perspire continually. The sun glares down scorching up the desert. And the unfortunate victims who are sufficiently misguided to live on it. The atmosphere is suffocating with absolutely no air.

I exist sans clothes, sans milk, eggs and butter and my greatest ambition is that the fly paper may become crowded, that it may chain fly after fly on its gluey surface, and I watch, fascinated as they die in torture.

The journey from Marseilles to Alexandria was a pleasant episode. The inevitable hiccup – cockroaches in cabin. My friend, Jessie Parnell, and I shared a cabin. She behaved nobly as she apparently did not mind cockroaches and took the lower bunk which saved me from brain fever.

We played most wholesome bridge and I realized my limitations. I play vilely. A rather pleasant person is on board, Captain Kelly. He was particularly nice to me and I did not know why until I arrived in this damned desert and found he had built the house Meyrick and I live in. Unfortunately, he built it so we would get the full force and glare of the sun.

Scorching sun and a following breeze on the Red Sea trip. Enormous cockroaches, not very amusing people, although I don't think on the Red Sea one could find anyone amusing or see humour in anything.

*Charlotte and Meyrick's House
in the Sudan 1907–08*

Charlotte (Lottie) back left playing tennis in Sudan

Arrived here I found husband Meyrick had made things as comfortable as possible. He was very pleased to see me. Thank heaven I cannot talk Arabic, and therefore Meyrick is doing the housekeeping. I do nothing all day, wear as little as possible and try to sleep as much as possible.

Some sinister insect got inside my riding breeches. I was stung on my back side and found a compounded corpse in the trouser lining. The sting turned to blood poisoning and I went to hospital in Khartoum to have a gland out.

Before this incident I had been ill, Red Sea fever, my temperature rose nightly, and I became weaker and weaker. I had been ordered on a milk diet but unable to cope with that which the Arab cook produced, chiefly watery blancmange, smelling of goats and made with goats' milk.

An Englishwoman, wife of a judge, heard of my plight and arrived with thermos flasks of nutriment– Nestles milk, cream, condiments from Fortnum and Mason, all perfectly packed. She certainly saved my life.

Large white ants made their nests in the walls of the house and had to be burned out.

The kitchen was unapproachable. Clouds of flies darkened the atmosphere and spiders were in every corner. Colossal spiders looking like large crabs. Quite unbelievable!

I remember taking a blue chiffon evening dress from a cupboard, seeing a large spider nestling in its folds, throwing the dress in horror on the bed.

At the same moment, a crowded flypaper detached from the ceiling and landed on my dress. The dress was then unapproachable and forever unwearable ... indeed the suitable costume for the Sudan would have been, and probably is today, brassiere and pants.

I have seen what appeared to be a tarantula under my full skirt and, in the agony of apprehension and to the great embarrassment of the assembled company, had to strip at lightning speed.

Despite these horrible bugs, there was some compensation society was good, but almost exclusively male.

December 31, 1909. Sudan

The end of 1909. I dare not say it has been a good year. I have not seen the mail today, so I have not had any news of those in England. There is only one post per week.

I have come to the conclusion that life is quite possible; only if one is surrounded by cases of tinned food from Fortnum and Mason and if one assuages one's thirst at every available opportunity with hock or claret, or oranges and ice backed up with gin. This latter is an excellent drink. Between drinks, I play bridge, tennis and sleep profoundly. I also horseback ride and sail.

Meyrick alarms me. He says I am under-mining his individuality. This is disastrous, more especially as his individuality is charming.

Yesterday morning a puppy that I had been trying in the face of difficulties to pull through distemper, showed signs of a severe relapse. Meyrick insisted that the puppy must be destroyed. Consequently, he persuaded me to have it sent to hospital where he swore it would be chloroformed.

This morning I become conscious on awakening of a considerable bustle proceeding in the bedroom. I asked what the matter was and sleepily heard that Nell, Meyrick's dog, had been lying on his bed. Ticks? I queried still sleepily. I was horrified, truly a nightmare!

"Ticks" Meyrick answered. Yes, hundreds and thousands of ticks. By then I was thoroughly awake.

Meyrick, with his kimono pinned round his knees, was sweeping the floor. The houseboy, Alnoubi, was removing bedding and the irritating little native boy was standing with open mouth, gaping stupidly.

I have since heard that Meyrick awoke to find Nell sleeping on the bed and the bed (his, thank heavens) black with ticks. They are cleaning out the room now with a totally inadequate supply of water, two buckets. It's a frightening experience.

I feel so cross and tired and quite a hundred years old. At present, death by drowning would appear attractive. I would like to swirl saturated and sink into fathoms of clear, clean water. I do not regret the puppy's death as his future would have chiefly consisted of providing meals for ticks.

Thank goodness my husband, Meyrick, left the Sudan Civil Service and went into his father's business back in London. We found a lovely flat which faced south and looked over Regents Park.

The move took time to be completed – even in those day when workmen and firms were able and anxious to do everything for one at the shortest possible notion.

Finally, after considerable expenditure, everything seemed in complete order and perfect; the future pleasant to look forward to. I seriously thought we were settled for life, with later on perhaps, a seaside cottage for the children and holidays.

My younger daughter, Rhoda, was two years old and I was expecting a third child, Meyrick (later known as Basil) when, suddenly and without warning the first world war was upon us. This shattered both present and future.

The newspaper baron, Northcliffe was as great a warmonger as Churchill. They had come into their own, with the power of the press and outright lies.

One afternoon I was having tea in Sloane Street. Several women were there. We heard the rhythm of music and the tramp of feet and looking out saw the street filled with marching men, young men marching to some station on their way to war.

It was terrible. They looked so young and hopeless. I knew that most of them were certainly going to be killed.

"Good, good" said one of the women, "This is what England needed; our young men were getting soft."

The woman's own son at that time was an infant. (Later, in the second World war, he was killed).

About this time (1913), Charlotte wrote the essay "The Militarist" and in late 1914 she wrote "Hades"; the first of her anti-war essays.

CHAPTER
NINE

Start of the First World War
1914, Aged 35

T he newspaper baron, Northcliffe, owner of the Daily Mail and Daily Mirror, as great a warmonger as Churchill. They had come into their own, with the power of the press and outright lies.

We, the ordinary people, did not know Northcliffe for what he was, a subhuman mental case. Many people believed the Times, Dairy Mail, etc. which declared Germany responsible for the war, stating that Germany insisted on war. Consequently, it seemed to the masses that Germany had forced the war and Britain had to fight. Britain's men were in a death trap.

Gradually, as the weeks went by, my eyes were opened. Many people in this country were war-minded and a great many were elated at the excitement of war.

Charlotte's husband was described by a fellow Army officer as "A shining light in sport and music at Wellington Col-

Meyrick Whitmore Payne
as Lt. Colonel in WW I

lege. He earned his B.A. with honors at Trinity College, Cambridge. He was 1 of 15 out of 60 selected for the prestigious Egyptian/Sudan Civil Service. He served as Deputy Inspector at Port Sudan on the Red Sea, as part of the British force overseeing access to the Suez Canal."

CHAPTER
TEN

Becoming a Pacifist
1915–1918, Aged 36–39

Sometime in 1915

The Liberal Party is now too insignificant to count. It was betrayed by two leaders: Chamberlain standing for tariff reform, and the war enthusiasm of Lloyd George.

In 1914, Europe was prosperous. There was goodwill everywhere; the prosperity of Britain was unlimited and wealth was enough to raise the standard of living and give good conditions everywhere.

When the 1914 war started, I had such faith in the Liberals that I believed they would leave no stone unturned to end the war, but when opportunities for a peace approach occurred, nothing happened. Then one became aware of an organized and growing clamor for more war and against peace.

In 1915, Bethmann-Hollweg, Chancellor of Germany, made a reasonable appeal for peace discussions but this appeal was summarily dismissed by the British Government. The continuation of the war after Germany's peace effort seemed to me the superlative injustice to young men everywhere.

My entire energy went into opposition and, incredibly, I found myself in a minority of one. Dislike, even hatred, was lavished upon me. I was called a peace crank. It was very confusing. I almost began to believe that I must be mad, and then I read that some women were going to Stockholm to urge peace and were forming a Woman's International League.

I went to their office and joined up. I began to read the socialist newspaper, "The Labour Leader," a very great paper in those days; the writers Snowdon, MacDonald, Trevelyan, Morel, Ponsonby, Russell and Mrs. Stanwick. Faith in my own sanity was restored and from that time on I called myself a pacifist and worked for the common sense of pacifism against the hypocrisy and neurosis of war.

Truth is war's first casualty; it is killed stone dead. Lies take its place suffocating the whole world's atmosphere which is choked with lies. Without the strength and support of Truth pacifism surely will be defeated.

We now know that all parties are equally responsible. War appears to them a game and they become like children playing at soldiers. G. B. Shaw suggested in a political treatise published much later, that the scope and power of politicians should be limited to home and local affairs. Foreign policy should be left to arbitration where those few of superlative qualifications, such as Nobel Prize winners, etc. decide.

My husband, Meyrick, enlisted in the Public School and University Corps. At that time, he believed that Germany was solely responsible for the war and that the British were a peace-loving people. I did not attempt to influence him.

Six months after the war started my son, Meyrick Fergus (known as Basil) was born. I had lost interest in my husband and my well-being.

To me, it seemed a sin to bring a son into the world when other mothers' sons were being slaughtered relentlessly. I gave up the flat in London and eventually moved down to Seafield.

Looking after three children left little opportunity for pacifist activity and I only distributed the magazine "Labour Leader." I did, however, incur notoriety.

Northcliff, owner of the right-wing Daily Mail and Daily Mirror, offered a reward to any county or town that would send up the name of local pacifists; North Devon must have sent up mine. I was the only avowed one in the district and consequently the police gave me all their attention. Letters were opened and various unpleasant incidents occurred.

August 1916

Thank God Meyrick has been appointed Staff Captain in Cork, Ireland. He started this morning. It gives him a chance of being alive after the war.

In the autumn of 1916, I distributed papers in favour of peace by negotiation. All the working women were in favour. One morning I was visiting houses near Waterloo Station and in one house I noticed a large picture of Horatio Bottomley, an advocate for war.

When the owner of the house saw my papers, she became a demon; she dashed into the street screaming she had a German there. With dignity I walked out. It was Saturday morning and the streets were full of children who gathered round and took up the cry, "She's a German, she's a German."

The crowd of children swelled swiftly. Passing a shop, I thought I would mollify them and tried to buy sweets, but sweets had lost their virtue, the clamor was too great. We reached a main street where stalls of a street market and crowded pavements disordered the procession, and there I leapt onto a tram.

August 5, 1916. Sandbanks, Dorset

I am going to Cork this next week to join Meyrick for three weeks. I trust I get over without being mined, torpedoed or bombed. I am taking Iris tomorrow to Motcombe, Priscilla's large house (aka Aunt Glad) to Miss Smith and am leaving Rhoda and baby here with Beatie, the nanny at Motcombe. Iris has learnt to swim well.

August 19, 1916. Imperial Hotel, Cork, Ireland

The journey here is long. I left Euston station at 8:30 am and arrived at Cork station at midnight. Meyrick met me. Cork is hideous. There is nothing to do, but fortunately there is a Carnegie library quite close.

December 4, 1916

Meyrick started a car trip on Saturday afternoon in the little Six and went to Killarney. Arrived there about 4 pm and went for a short walk in the grounds of Lord Kenmare's place. It has been destroyed by fire, but the grounds are beautiful, palms and other tropical plants growing luxuriantly.

After a very good dinner and a very good night despite a very hard bed, started the next day for Waterville. The road alongside the Killarney lakes is beautiful.

Having climbed to the top of the mountains over the other side we got our first glimpse of the Atlantic and later got onto the road known as the Great Atlantic Route which runs alongside the inlet of ocean for thirty miles.

We had lunch at Waterville and came back the same way. It is the most unique coastline, tropical woods and forests right down to the water's edge and the water in these great big harbors and inlets, although it is the Atlantic, calm and serene.

It is really very like the Riviera and enterprising Germans before the war ran an excellent hotel here.

Of course, in the present disordered national outlook, the owners are supposed to have done this entirely to help the Germans' impending military struggle. It seems far more probable to me that they did it from the point of a good speculation.

The native population live in squalid, broken-down huts which are a disgrace to the scenery. As usual nature has done her best for man and man's sense of gratitude has not come uppermost.

December 31, 1916. Nearly midnight, Dorset

1917, or at least on the eve of it. One dare not really look ahead; feels as if one were being thrust forward to the edge of an abyss. It only needs another three months to complete three years of wholesale slaughter. The non-combatants hounding on the young men and insisting that they shall slaughter and be slaughtered.

My brother Fergus is in the firing line in France. He hates the war, loathes the army, but is the victim of circumstance as are thousands of others.

Meyrick, thank God, is in Cork, surrounded by non-combatants in uniform who want the war to go on forever. Many of Meyrick's and my best friends have been killed. Terrible!

January 20, 1917

I have brought the children from Motcombe house to Canford Cliffs, near Bournemouth.

Priscilla produced a play of her own writing this week. Everyone worked strenuously, but I hear that the acting crowd, "The Shaftsbury," people resent the expense they invested on the seats. They were certainly a cold audience. I was in the orchestra, with a local gas fitter who played the violin quite nicely.

March 9, 1917. Savoy Hotel, London

Woke up this morning to find appalling blizzard blowing down here in north Devon. Not one of fires would burn and smoke poured down the chimneys.

I postponed going up to London till the wind changed as I felt could not leave my family enveloped in smoke. Eventually I caught the 1:57 pm from Westbourne. In the train I talked about the futility of war as usual. There was one sound supporter, the rest rather too scared to voice what they thought.

Arrived Savoy, had a delightful suite. Very nice tea and luxurious one despite shrieks for economy from every side.

Dined with Priscilla and Fergus at St. James' Palace. Fergus is so war weary, he hates talking of the war, but he is so frightfully ignorant of facts as they are, one cannot let it rest at that.

On my return here found a most horrible woman had opened my letters from Meyrick. There might possibly have been an excuse for opening one, but as the second was addressed in the same way and in the same writing, she could only have done it out of spite and vindictive curiosity.

April 19, 1917. Cork

The weather has been very pleasant here. A motor run every afternoon.

Yesterday we went to Fermoy and Lismore. The country is beautiful everywhere, but it is not populated. Ruined cottages and ruined castles everywhere. And when the latter are not in ruins, they are not occupied.

Everything here is going to ruin and decay. This country really is an indictment on men's policy. It has every possibility and every possible asset to content the mind of man and make his life pleasant. Man has squandered capital and made himself and the country bankrupt.

The life of the individual is of enormous value to the world and it is the negation of this fact which is at the bottom of the failure of civilization.

Continuous slaughter is going on at the Western front.

The German official report calls it the greatest battle in history. So demoralizing has been the effect of the past three years that even I, with Fergus in the thick of it, am acquiring again the calm of a normal mind. The incessant shock and horror of men killing each other is wearing me down. I am growing used to it.

May 12, 1917

I was fined on May 7th 20 pounds for showing lights during the blackout. This is a quite unusual fine and I think it was instigated because I am known to hold pacifist views.

May 20, 1917

Ireland's state is deplorable. It is one of inertia and waste.

Presumably it is the consistent policy of passive resistance to English government. The people are determined not to attempt to do or be their best under English rule. As this has been going on for years, the country and people have been consistently on the downward slope.

They have lost hope and, robbed of self-respect, have taken to drink. They have become an easy prey for the Catholic Church which, without opposition of any kind, has educated them and influenced them in the lies and fallacies of its creed.

Those who have read history, or Eugene Sue's *The Wandering Jew* or Zola's *Lourdes* and *Rome*, understand the subtlety and cunning of the Machiavellian method that the ends justifies the means.

June 1, 1917

Funny thing. I have had various dreams of Zeppelins and the dangers of them, but I have never felt worried about them. I mean, felt any worry of danger to myself.

Well, Meyrick and I are back in London – Meyrick has been offered a job in the Sudan and consequently has left Cork.

Yesterday morning, after having visited the War Office, we taxied to Meyrick's bank. I sat in the taxi outside, grilling in the sun, while he proceeded to do business. Suddenly I heard a far distant explosion and thought "a munitions factory explosion." A few seconds later I heard similar sound much nearer and began to think less lethargically. Bombs!

Then, suddenly behind and before me came two colossal explosions. I leapt from the cab, men's faces were blanch and questioning. I think I heard someone say, "Take cover!" It was only a moment before I flung myself into the bank.

Inside they did not realize things, but the door swung open again and a dozen terrified girls raced in asking whether they might go down to the cellars.

I went down with them, but Meyrick refused to remain below, so I also emerged and a few minutes later we got into our taxi and drove homeward.

The morning papers say that 97 were killed and 439 injured, 26 children killed and 94 injured. They dropped thirteen bombs on the City. We were in the thick of it.

July 4, 1917. Seafield

Meyrick was given leave by the War Office prior to his departure for the Sudan.

We accordingly came down here, the whole family and Bino, for the first few days. It has been a very perfect interlude (touch wood) in the third year of war. It seems almost necessary to take one's mind off the war when at any moment a wire may come for Meyrick and take him to Sudan where he may or may not arrive sans disaster.

This is our third week down here and we are all very robust, well filled with ozone and Devonshire cream.

Westward-Ho disguises the tragedy of war. On the sands there are only two men (boatmen), Hoare and Wadis. The former has lost his two splendid sons – both killed. Wadis' son was wounded severely, first in the Dardanelles then in France, and this year he was sent to China.

Since his departure his wife was confined, and she and the baby died. Wadis and Hoare are both in their eighties and it is a tragedy to see them doing the work that their sons should be there to do for them.

July 23, 1917. Seafield, Westward Ho, North Devon

I went down to Southampton and saw Meyrick off. He hated going and quite broke down when he said goodbye to the children. We had several cocktails in the hotel in Southampton which helped us both enormously. You cannot say goodbyes these dreadful days unless you are stupefied with drink and tobacco.

November 11, 1918. Armistice Day

We were at Seafield on November 11, 1918. I had a cook and governess working for me, both elderly women receiving substantial financial contributions from male relatives engaged in war work.

When they were told of the armistice, they were disappointed, irritable, said, "Of course, it isn't true!!!"

To me the relief of tension seemed incredible. The war was over. It was a gray morning. The unending, murmurous roar of the waves, the acrid scent of gorse along the cliffs. One had to celebrate. I met soldiers and airmen. Generosity was a gesture to later libation – Perpetual Peace and Goodwill. We laughed that morning, tears behind the laughter.

After the First World War

After the 1914 war my moral standards deteriorated. I had no sympathy for the old, they had seemed so complacent during the war years. Miss Lennard (Lussy), our housekeeper, had married and had been out of our lives for many years.

She wrote that her husband had died, and she asked for financial help.

She was eighty and in difficulties and I ought to have done my best to help her. I sent her 5 pounds and that was all. I forgot about her and only remembered her later when I heard that she had died in a workhouse.

Explanatory note by CMP. During a long period after WW I Charlotte stopped writing her diary. Instead she wrote a series of essays decrying the folly of WW I.

Daughter Rhoda's Story: Charlotte's Love in WW I

This is a First World War story told by Charlotte's daughter, Rhoda Lawrence.

My mother, Charlotte, had rented her brother's house, Seafield, in Westward Ho! North Devon.

It was the early days of the war and my father was in Egypt serving in with the Sudan Civil Service. So, we left London and went down to North Devon taking with us a wonderful woman called Beatie. She was our Nanny, but my mother could not stand that name as it reminded her of goats!

My sister, Iris, was eight, I was four and Basil was one. Seafield was situated at the end along a gravel road, perched at the edge of a cliff. The house was at the side of the Bay. It was very isolated as there were no other houses on the road. When the tide came in over the rocks below our gardens the sea would splash against the rocks. The spray would land on our windows.

After living in London, us children thought this wonderful.

As the house was too large for the five of us the top floors were shut. This made the uppermost windows easy to black out. But unfortunately, the ones nearer the ground and on the second floor were Victorian and very hard to open although Beatie did her best to close them. Even with sturdy blankets it was difficult not to show lights; especially when gales of wind whipped around the house.

Unfortunately, my mother was very keen on fresh sea air, especially sea air, and would insist on opening our bedroom windows. Basil often felt sick in the night and would yell for help causing Charlotte to spring out of bed and switch on the light and rush to his assistance, quite forgetting about the blackout.

This led to considerable trouble with the police. After it happened several times, they thought she was sending signals to the Germans out at sea. This was not altogether surprising because everyone knew of her strong antiwar feelings. Our prams and sandcastles on the beach always flew the red flag, a sure sign of socialism and protest.

I remember asking her why. She told me that we were internationalists and the world was our country; and that was that!

My sister, Iris, faced the brunt of our unpopularity. She attended the village school where no one spoke to her. Despite this we managed to settle ourselves in a pattern at Seafield. We were comparatively happy and comfortable. Thanks largely to Beatie who did everything.

In the morning she would walk an unwilling Iris up the gravel road to the village school. Every afternoon my mother would push Basil and I to the beach where Iris would join us after school.

On one such day we made friends with a lovely black Labrador dog who greeted us with wagging tail and great enthusiasm. His master was young and paused to admire our sandcastles before taking off across the beach. Now and then he threw sticks into the sea for his dog to retrieve. Eventually master and dog would disappear into the distance.

When they returned looking hot and tired my mother offered him a cup of tea from our picnic basket. He and the dog sat down on the rug with us. We had a very happy time.

When we left the beach each evening, he pushed the pram up the slope to the road for my mother. When we went our separate ways, he said "can we meet here again tomorrow?" We all shouted "yes" at the same time.

After a few days we became very fond of Valour, the dog and his master. Every day after their walk, they would join us with our picnic. We began to add water in a bottle for the thirsty dog. Sometimes the nice man would help us build sandcastles; sometimes he would just lie back on the rug gazing at the sky and just talk.

One day he was late coming to the beach. When he arrived, he looked so different that we hardly recognized him. He was in a Royal Air Force uniform. As always Valour was walking at his heel, but for once he was wearing a collar.

I don't think we even said goodbye to this young man we had grown to love so much. He sat Valour down on the rug beside my mother. He told Valour to stay. Then pulling a lead out of his pocket he attached it to the collar. He handed the leash to my mother.

When he walked away, he never looked back. Valour sat with his ears pricked as his master walked away. Valour started to whimper. I looked at my mother and saw tears running down her cheeks. Iris and I started to cry too.

It was a very sad family that walked back to Seafield that night. Valour did not want to leave the beach. We had to pull on his leash.

Valour thought he should wait where he had been left by his master, who would surely return as usual.

We had dreadful weeks with a broken-hearted dog. He would not eat and howled ceaselessly. My mother kept him in her room at night to try and stop him keeping everyone awake. We all tried giving him our rationed meat and sweets. Valour refused them all. He became thin and his coat lost its shine.

A very long time passed before Valour became resigned to living with us. But eventually this happened, and he became devoted to my mother, whose side he never left. Valour grew to love us all and we loved him. He had him for 12 years.

During that time if we ever heard a gunshot, he would prick his ears and gaze into the distance. Valour would sigh deeply and lie down to sleep.

Such was life and death in wartime.

Grandson Meyrick's Story:
How Charlotte Lost Her Family's Fortune

A Story passed down to CMP over many years (and probably exaggerated).

Charlotte's brother, Bino, was, as the family stories are told, a wealthy undergraduate at Trinity College at Cambridge University in the late nineteenth century.

Bino lived in rooms above the main gate to Trinity College, from which he had a wonderful view down Cambridge High Street. About 1898, he was bored by his studies. Looking down the High Street he noticed several workmen digging up the road. Bino was, by reputation, a troublemaker.

He went down to the workmen and said "Listen, I'm sorry to have to tell you, but a bunch of undergraduates are coming to stop you doing your job."

He then went to the police station and said, "I think you ought to know that there's a bunch of undergraduates digging up the road outside Trinity Gate."

Bino returned to his rooms and watched the ensuing fight! That was Bino.

How Charlotte lost her family fortune is a sad story. At the beginning of the First World War Charlotte and her family were moderately well off. But Charlotte was very much on her own financially.

Her mother and father had died before she turned twenty five. Her diary reveals that she was very much aware of the need to find a suitable mate. The one she found, Meyrick Whitmore Payne, (my Grandfather) was charming but no better off than herself.

In the first years of World War I, her stockbroker advised her to sell out her inherited investments in Russian steel and railroads, which were principally centered around the city of Stalino, now Donetsk, in Ukraine.

Unfortunately, the stockbroker could not find a buyer until late 1916 when he wrote to tell her that, miracle of miracles, he had a buyer. She sold everything.

Well it turned out that the buyer was brother Bino who believed in the philosophy of Karl Marx. What is more, he pledged the family fortune as collateral for the purchase of Charlotte's shares. In March 1917, along came the Russian revolution and all was lost!

Bino was man enough to admit his tragic error and vowed to live in poverty from then on.

As it was WW I, the Germans had dropped bombs from gliders over much of England. One of these gliders had crashed on Salisbury Plain in Southern England. Bino lived in it for several years! Of course, his siblings took pity on him and he became a frequent long-term guest. Filial love has no bounds!

And that is how Charlotte's family fortune was lost.

ESSAYS

The Militarist; Exposing Pro-World War I Bellicose Propaganda

Abstract by CMP. Charlotte hated war. She hated militarist propaganda equally. Women seemed to her as the loudest advocates of nationalism and war.

The Militarists have come into their own. We see them unmasked and we hear them shouting from the housetops. Men and women, we find them, in all grades of society, their faces flushed with the virtue of patriotism, expounding their obnoxious ideas. Germany has her bellicose General Bernhardi, England has Colonel Colin (Mad) Maude. It is because one feels the pernicious effect of the spread of their false ideas, that the pacifist is forced to come forward and refute them.

A knowledge of relative values is a science which has been grossly neglected. It is the essence of education and no fine sense of justice can be formed without it. The Militarist is a neurotic. He has no sense of proper values. He says that to die for one's country is the fine thing. He acclaims that the life of the individual counts for nothing, He is generally non-combatant and is emphatic on the point that he does not mind what sacrifice the war entails.

To their everlasting disgrace, it must be admitted that there are many women militarists. Though some fantastic mental process they give refinements to the blood lust and confess their satisfaction that men can still die for ideas.

In England, the influence of the militarist is rampant, Horatio Bottomley and Mrs. Pankhurst lead public opinion. Badly maimed and injured men are kept out of the way in barracks, so that they will not influence the recruiting for war.

The atrocities of Belgium have been rehashed and heroic pictures are distributed gratis at the post office to influence public thought in a pro-war direction. Propaganda!

I went into a children's nursery school this week. On the walls were hanging recruiting posters: Britannia with a sword unsheathed shouting, to the children apparently, "Remember Belgium."

A book has been written by Emile Zola called "J 'Accuse." The writer has taken Zola's historic phrase in calling the combatants to account. I would like to bring that phrase home to all Militarists., journalists, women and the Church.

It is about 30 years since Huxley, Tyndale and other great thinkers were at the zenith of their fame. They followed up the teachings of Voltaire and Darwin and wrote clear, concise Truth.

Public opinion was against them. They were execrated as atheists, but their books were read and those who read them became under their influence: their words were sane and wholesome.

Years have intervened. I doubt very much, if many of the younger generation have read the teachings of those men who did their best to prove that orthodox religion is a pernicious influence that as, Alexander Kinglake wrote, "Faith is the power of believing things we know to be untrue."

Ignorance and superstition have again obtained influence. In place of rationalism, we have the mirage of spiritualism gaining ground on the horizon.

Theosophists, Christian Scientists and elderly scientists assure us of knowledge of those who have left this world.

Behind these lesser evils we have the creeds, in England and German the protestant Church exerts an enormous influence, especially on women.

In reply to the question: "Has the Church failed in the present crisis?"

The Church answers "The souls of men, not their bodies, are our business!"

The Church is consistent in believing in the glories of a hereafter. Consequently, Death is a blessing.

They hardly admit horror, in the present wartime situation, they see suffering and death as a purifying force giving entrance to heaven.

The Church, however, cannot have it both ways and admitting that her altitude towards the war is consistent, with her creed.

The Church becomes illogical in her assertion that war is a form of redemption for the world.

We should recognize that orthodox religion is an appreciation of the world's ruin.

Happiness and health are negation of sin and disease and, as such, do not bring the "blessings" of death and consequently, the spiritual existence, nearer to the individual.

The time is almost ripe for an enormous religious revival. Human nature does not adapt well to despair. Hope is a sensation which is less painful.

The Church offers the compensation of Death and because people have nothing left worth living for. In desperation people tend to believe the Church.

The Germans are accused of having no sense of humor. It may be that deficiency which lead them with "pomp and circumstance" to march out to ruin Europe.

England under the influence of the militarists has lost her sense of humour; as such she fails to see the absurdity of war. She is inclined to give praise to war, as a fine and gracious thing.

We live today in an atmosphere of humbug.

The militarist decides, what we shall know, just that and no more. He dwells on the horrors of Belgium; the women raped, and the children mutilated but omits to add that the German women and children have suffered in the same way.

History repeats itself. In all wars, these things have happened. It is part and parcel of the whole filthy business.

It was to help necessary for England to stop Germany's onrush and to fulfill her guarantee to Belgium. It is equally necessary for England to attempt to restore law and order in Europe.

England should have the moral courage to suggest arbitration, as an alternative to the unendurable continuation of the martyrdom of men.

Charlotte E. Nixon Payne

Hades, the Hell of the First World War

Abstract by CMP. War is Hell and those who make it happen are devils; war is often induced by excessive patriotism and nationalism. Arbitration and appeasement is so much preferable to war and the death of millions of young people.

At first it seemed a nightmare. Germany and Austria had been guilty of the crass stupidity of starting a European war. They had had the temerity to overthrow civilization. The avalanche of war had started on its overwhelming, crushing journey, and one realized the disasters ahead.

Germany's exaggerated patriotism welds at the root of the trouble and her wish to acquire fresh territory, also her militarism which had turned the county's manhood into an efficient fighting machine.

Ten months of war have given, from a military point of view, only negative results. Devastation and death are everywhere, but this, from a military point of view, does not count.

One might have thought that the need to attain justice was desirable and the futility of war clearly proved. The one definite result is the spread of the war fever which started Germany on her suicidal course. Patriotism has now usurped the place of common sense and the wish to acquire new territory is not confined to Germany.

To me the impression is that the inhabitants of the world, most especially Europe, have gone raving mad. No one attempts to be consistent in their theories and logic is lost sight of.

"Lord Roberts was right; we should have had conscription." "Germany must be crushed and pulverized, because of her militarism." "The war, as the Germans wage it, is not war – it is murder."

In the tenth month of the war, the Government urges that England should organize for an additional output of munitions, and the country begins to understand that war is serious.

Germany can use ammunition freely, while England and France, owing to an insufficiency of shells, are allowing their manhood to be slaughtered in additional thousands without response.

Germany is the foremost military power of the world today, and

Germany has shown the world that in war conventions are, one and all, untenable.

War is the heinous crime – the unforgivable error. Great Britain had been guilty of irresponsibility, she should either, as Germany has turned her manhood into an efficient fighting machine; or taken measures to ensure coalition support by international force prescribed under the Hague tribunal and its conventions.

The Hague Tribunal stands as the Court of Arbitration for international disputes and England should have given it her support by declaring war, as an alternative, (has committed) the greatest crime.

In the meanwhile, we have the world of today. England and Germany both asserting that they are waging war in the name of civilization. The Germans declaring this a war of aggression against Germany; the Allies declaring it a war of aggression against them.

Panic and patriotism have done their worst. No one stops to reason. The great avalanche rolls, crushing youth, women and children in its train. And the greatest irony is that everyone is supposed not to mind. Salvation is not to be attempted; we are to welcome death and disaster with smiling faces and outstretched hands. This is supposed to be patriotism. Above the din everyone is shouting justice. No sacrifice is too great for justice and one's country. They forget that every day of the war is undermining the future of Europe.

On all sides we see the crippled and the maimed. Blind men are guided by philanthropic helpers through our streets and parks. English women labor enthusiastically, and often inadequately, for the victims of war. Draped in crepe and beads the widows chatter gaily in the sunshine.

Women say our men are dying gloriously, and that consequently it is the civilian's duty to be cheered – so despite universal mourning women continue a lighthearted course. The shops and theaters are doing their usual trade, and thousands of people are kept employed on things that may please women's fancy in their "joie de vivre."

Splendid women they have accepted with philosophic calm (a large proportion of them) the burial of Europe's best manhood. While the virtuous are doing they duty in England, others are on the continent contributing their quota in the devil's scheme of general disorganization.

The papers except for the Daily Mail, which has detached itself in the last two months from the other's jubilant press, clamor of the victorious progress of the Allies. The German radio and press speak of heavy losses of the enemies and sanguinary encounters.

People say it is "Impossible to believe the German accounts," but the casualty lists, although they are made as indefinite as print will allow, support the German claims. "The Tatler" and "The Sketch," etc. have the ladies of the Stage and Society broadly smiling on one side and the Roll of Honour on the other.

Germany's superiority in guns and munitions is an effective reply to those who say that Germany must be stamped out as vermin and that, as a nation, she must cease to exist. If we curse ourselves for our folly in not having had conscription, how can we condemn Germany's army. England has been blind and now is paying the price.

It is the stupidity of not realizing the evil of war which we should condemn. Since the war started, however, I have met so many fools in England who talk of war as if it was a blessing in disguise, that one realizes criminal lunacy is not confined to Germany. Nations in future must protect themselves against the folly of the individual.

Surely England should negotiate a peace before all manhood is dead.

Justice, the First World War in Perspective

Abstract by CMP. War starts by mistake but then can't be stopped. The combatants at first recognize that arbitration would be preferable but when men die, they become locked in a tit-for-tat battle until millions are dead.

That civilization has not taken steps to safeguard herself from war is a mistake which civilization will admit when, in the cool calm of future day, history condemns us.

There was only one way to avert this disaster, the International Tribunal at the Hague should have been backed by International Force.

Looking back, Austria should have been made to submit her grievances with Serbia to the International Tribunal at the Hague, and, if Germany had supported her in a refusal, the civilized world should have brought all its forces to bear against these two "recalcitrant powers."

Germany's violation of the League of Nations Conventions was an international matter.

The Neutral Countries should have accepted their share of the responsibility in August 1914 when Belgium's neutrality was violated. It is an injustice towards the Allies that they did not do so.

War, as an alternative to arbitration, is a fool's game and leads from confusion to confusion worse confounded.

Sixteen years ago, England declared the Boer war on the Transvaal. The wrongs of the "Uitlanders" and the various matters which led up to the war are immaterial and were at the time relatively unimportant.

The reason why England acted as she did was because she would not submit the points under discussion to arbitration.

The meaning of war is to kill as many of the enemy as possible for the sake of one's own side, friends and brothers, to put them "hors de combat."

Wholesale slaughter becomes the objective of millions of individuals. It is simply murder, and murder justified by the strong instinct of self-preservation.

If you do not kill the enemy, he will kill you. Combatants thrust on blindly, viciously, obedient to the life instinct and the fools who have ordered the killing.

Whether a man is killed, ripped up by a bayonet or has his brains bashed out by the butt end of a rifle, there is little to choose from between the agony and method of either process.

Men see red and, fighting for their lives, there is no time for fine distinctions.

It has taken a great deal to make the people of England know what war means. The sinking of the Lusitania and the accounts of the effects on our men of gassing seem at last to have done so and made them realize the injustice of unnatural death.

Some now say that "this is not war," not what they understand by war.

In Christ's name, what did they expect? If you are out to kill the man who is out to kill you, you must leave as little as possible to chance.

The civilian of today may be the soldier of tomorrow and therefore, arguing from a war basis, everything is justifiable.

There is no justice in war.

We have now had nine months of unparalleled suffering and bloodshed, thousands, millions of young men are dead.

Women are widows and children fatherless.

Everybody is in mourning. As one moves along the streets, one catches one's breath in horror.

It seems that war on this gigantic scale means extermination of all that is good and fine in the Nation. I think it does mean this. Rather than outraged Nature and Gods, the bird's eye view of the world at present would show man, like an unreasoning child destroying everything, himself included.

Balancing the largest view of things, it is immaterial that the Allies are wholly in the right, that our cause is just. Germany is the aggressor. It is God's world that we bring our children into. And man has spoiled it.

People have always underrated the value of life. They have also overrated the Compensation of Death.

Religion is misleading. Possibilities of a future life confuse thoughts. It would be better if man had taken this world as God's Heavens, he then possibly, would have avoided turning it into Hell.

It has always seemed to me that men and the world, in relation to each other are complete without the promise of an afterlife.

There is be no justice in giving man another life.

It is man's injustice to God that makes him expect a hereafter.

International patriotism could be a fine thing. In normal times everything is international, trade and finance.

These great arteries of civilization must be international to be succesful. People talk glibly of the past and their folk lore.

One does not realize the tragedies of past generations. Taking the wars that are nearest to our own time, the Boer and Crimea war stand out as the ultimate foolishness.

The British activity in the latter, we must now acknowledge, at least, as an error of judgment.

France, although defeated in the Crimea, only suffered a fraction of what she is enduring now.

The real history of war has never been written. At a future date, the history should be by the doctors who have been on the battle fields of

Europe. And a scientist should write the sequel shoving the direct effect of wholesale slaughter and suffering upon the nation.

England is now the throes of fervent patriotism. Patriotism that borders on dementia. It is chiefly evidenced by the noncombatants who say that at all cost, no matter the sacrifice, we must fight to the end.

The means to that end are the bodies of those young men, who have so far survived the debacle of youth.

Each one will go through to the end unswerving and silent but each one would give his soul that the necessity for sacrifice might be removed.

Cannot statesmen and other great men become less proud and sustain justice for the remaining youth of a mistaken world?

Defeat Peace at Any Price; The Duplicity of Peace Efforts During WW I

Abstract by CMP. Charlotte enumerates the efforts in WW I for peace which were illogically rejected by the Allied powers out of a desire to preserve their own empires and to punish Germany to the extent that its colonial possessions can be distributed among the Allies. Charlotte recalls that the punitive Treaty of Versailles directly led to WW II.

The figures of recent elections are incredible. The Government supported by the Labour Party is spending seven millions per day of the people's money, the money that should provide a fine standard of living for them all, yet, in spite of this and the fact that the majority of the workers are badly housed and cannot afford a good life, they cast their vote in favour of the continuation of the war and their consequent complete ruin.

As in all wars, the people believe and are led by the press and its inaccuracy. The Hitler panic covers their horizon.

Looking through my diary 1914–1919, it is pathetic to read, time after time, how every hope of Peace was lost and every chance for Peace defeated.

On December 10, 1915, In the Reichstag the German Chancellor suggests no annexation by conquest and asks for guarantees for Germany's safety.

Why in Heaven's name, can't we discuss Peace now but alas, the glamour and appreciation of war, rises on all sides.

February 1916. Snowdon, Trevelyan and Ponsonby stated the case for Peace. Asquith in a flood of rhetoric and supported by the House, turned them down.

All through, those dreadful years, whenever a possibility of peace was rumored. The Press shouted and the people echoed that Peace was premature.

In a pamphlet published by the W.D.C. in 1918, the nine overtures for peace and their rejections are enumerated.

First Peace Opening in December 1916. Enemy powers propose conference.

On December 12, 1916, the German Chancellor announces in the Reichstag that the Central Powers had proposed "This morning to the Hostile Powers to enter into Peace negotiations – former declarations of willingness to negotiate had been evaded – hence a formal offer is now put forward."

Second Peace Opening December 1916. President Wilson issues note to all belligerents that a change of views would clear the way at least for a conference to end the war.

The Central Powers welcomed the note and proposed immediate meeting of delegates of the belligerent states at some neutral location.

The Allies, England, France and Russia, all registered a further rejection of all proposals to meet the enemy at a conference aimed at ending the war.

Third Peace Opening March 1917. Private efforts of King Karl and the public overtures of the Austrian/Hungarian Governments advocating peace.

Count Tiza, the Hungarian Premier, declares that "We are still prepared to negotiate as soon as we have a guarantee that our enemies are willing to negotiate with us to attain such a Peace as proposed by President Wilson."

Fourth Peace Opening 1917. Efforts of first Russian revolutionary government, the Provisional Government, adopts openly as its aim the establishment of a general peace agreement based on "A Peace without annexations with indemnities for the participants based on the rights of nations to decide their own destinies."

Fifth Peace Opening August 1917. The Resolution of the German Reichstag Resolution.

"As in August 1914 (the start of the First World War) and now in the fourth year of war, the motivation of the German Government is "Solely for the benefit of the German people. We are not impelled by lust of conquest; but rather for the defense of German freedom and Independence, and for the integrity of her territorial possessions, Germany went to war. The Reichstag today strives for a peace of understanding and the permanent reconciliation of the embattled peoples.

With such a peace forced acquisition of territory and political, economic, or financial oppression is inconsistent. The Reichstag also rejected all schemes which aim at economic barriers and hostility between peoples. After the war, only economic peace will prepare the ground for a friendly intercourse between the nations."

This resolution passed, unnoticed by the British Public; the Manchester Guardian was probably the only paper that published it and Mr. Lloyd George made no allusion to it at the time.

Sixth Peace Opening, August 1, 1917. The Pope's Appeal.

The Pope urged an agreement regarding reduction of armaments, arbitration, total evacuation of Belgium, evacuation of the occupied parts of France and the restoration of German Colonies and dignity.

The Appeal says "Reflect upon your grave responsibility before God and before Man; Upon your decision depends the comfort and joy of innumerable families, the life of thousands of young people, the happiness in a world of the nations whose wellbeing, it is your absolute duty to procure peace."

The Central Powers replied approving the Pope's step and hoped that a suitable basis would be found for initiating negotiations with a view to preparing a peace accord, which was just to all and lasting. The Pope earnestly hoped our present enemies may be animated by the same ideas.

The Allied Governments returned no reply to the Pope's Appeal.

The technical rejection was contained in Article 15 of the Secret Treaty with Italy and reading as follows:

"France, Great Britain and Russia pledge themselves to support Italy in not allowing the Representatives of the Holy See to undertake any steps whatsoever in the matter of the conclusion of peace or the settlement of questions connected with the present war."

Seventh Peace Opening in 1917. German Government Overtires.

The German Government, through the intermediary of a Belgian diplomat, approached Aristide Briand, the former prime Minister of France, with a view to opening peace negotiations.

On October 11, 1917 the Reuters press Agency wrote:

"The essence of what may be described as peace talk is well understood among the Allies to be a direct result of the latest military developments in Flanders and Mesopotamia. The end of this war is only legitimately achieved by the sword."

Eight Peace Opening on November 22, 1917.

The Russian Bolshevik Government addressed a note to all diplomatic representatives of the Powers during their meeting in Petrograd, proposing:

"An immediate Truce upon all the fronts and to take immediate steps to get started on negotiations for Peace."

This outreach was not responded to by the Allied Powers. England and France completely disassociated themselves from any negotiations.

Ninth Peace Opening January 1918.

President Wilson again intervenes by a direct appeal to Germany and Austria to open a public discussion. He elaborated a Peace programme of 14 clauses.

Germany and Austria welcome this initiative for negotiations toward Peace.

The reply of the Allied Governments was included in a declaration from the Supreme War Council at Versailles.

"The Supreme War Council gave the most careful consideration to the recent utterances of the German Chancellor and of the Austro-Hungarian minister for Foreign Affairs but was unable to find in them any real approximation to the moderate conditions laid down by the Allied Governments.

"The Allies are united in heart and not by any hidden designs, but by their open resolve to defend civilization against an unscrupulous and brutal attempt at domination."

This rhetoric was totally misleading and disguised the unstated war aims of England and France.

All overtures for Peace were defeated.

Millions of men, hoping for salvation were ruthlessly slaughtered.

War is an opportunity for fools and knaves, who form their invincible combine to defeat Peace at any price.

Public opinion was led by Lord Northcliffe and Horatio Bottomley. At the end of the war, Northcliffe was certified as a lunatic. Bottomley was in prison for forgery and other crimes.

The British people should reflect and not allow lies to reap their full harvest as in World War I.

CHAPTER ELEVEN

Stresses and Strains of Family Life After WW I
1919–1930, Aged 40–51

"Life, a short glimpse between eternity, no second chance for us forever more." Carlyle.

My husband survived the war. Most of our friends had been killed. A few came back defeated – Jack Ken with a wooden leg; he tried to maintain normality to show that a wooden leg was of no consequence, but after a few years of sustained effort he shot himself.

Then there was Jim Leyton and his two brothers. Their parents had died when they were young and Jim had taken over parental responsibilities. In France both brothers were killed, one in the trench besides Jim. When he returned to England, he courted death recklessly; he had not the slightest wish to live, and when he became ill with pneumonia he died with no regrets as his friends knew. So many crucified.

There was a boy of twenty, beautiful as a Greek God, son of our landlady in rooms in London. He had been shot through the head and some part of the lead remained and could not be extracted. He had bouts of pain and as the months passed, these grew in intensity till they became unbearable and death ended intolerable living.

I thought we never could get over the losses of those years, never laugh lightheartedly again. But time is inexorable and the powers of recuperation immense in humanity; all this time the children were growing up.

Early 1919. Greyfriars, Tilford, Surrey

I have bought a house for 5,000 pounds – Greyfriars, Tilford, Surrey but the purchase is not complete until the end of May.

June 12, 1919

Traveled here from Westward Ho in guards van of the train, with dogs and cats. Found painters here as well as Harrods' furniture movers. Mrs. Smith and Chapman dazed with the consequent chaos.

Written later by Charlotte: In 1919, we bought a smallish place in Surrey forty-three miles from London – "ideal for children and dogs" as a sister-in-law summed it up one day after we had walked over the heather common and round our lovely lake. Today, (about 1948) it is significant the change the second world war made for the lake is gone, its waters drained like the Crystal Palace as it might, as they say, have guided German planes to London. The great pine trees are cut down, all part of the general blackout, the extinction of good by evil.

Back to the diary – My small boy, Meyrick (Basil) had Spanish influenza in the last war summer of 1918. He had acute anemia and doctors said he would not recover; but slowly, gradually, he regained his health.

Through the years, life at Greyfriars suited me. It was peace and tranquility of order despite children, chickens, dogs and cats, etc.

June 18, 1919

Basil was left at Farnbrough Station by Mrs. Hammond and I met him. He looked very anemic but seemed otherwise all right. However, three days later he was running a high temperature at night, but he seemed all right in the mornings. It was not until Monday morning when I took his temperature and found it 101 that I sent for the doctor. He was very ill, and the doctor seemed uncertain what was wrong with him.

Next day, Tuesday, after examination of his blood, he diagnosed it as splenic anemia and Dr. Couchman, who came round in the evening, said that there was no doubt that it was this and it was a fatal complaint as people did not respond to treatment and consequently there was no hope of recovery.

He said all this in a casual, everyday sort of way and mentally gave me such a shock that I sounded the depths of despair and remained there throughout the night. In the morning before 8 am, I telephoned Priscilla who wired overnight that she would bring a specialist doctor down. I told her that the case was not urgent, but the doctor had said the illness was fatal.

They arrived at 12 pm, Basil was in a high fever and the local Doctor Gool-May gave it as his opinion that he would not recover, but said that sometimes with children while there is life there is hope and told me to wire husband Meyrick that Basil was seriously ill.

Basil has been running a high fever for about a week but from that day his temperature gradually went down, and he has responded to treatment splendidly. He has a pink colour and the blood has come back to his fingertips, etc. On examination, his blood was found to be much better. Dr. Tanner, another local doctor, is a very clever man and a convincing one. He said that he always thought Basil would get over it and he says his progress is quite satisfactory.

November 10, 1920. Greyfriars

It is nearly eighteen months, since I have written in this diary.

Greyfriars suits me very well and the children, thank God, are flourishing. Basil is now robust and Dr. May and Dr. Tanner both express the opinion that he is no longer anemic.

Meyrick has a flat in London and I go twice a week. We have a car which helps us through a divided and somewhat difficult existence. Now one is strangled financially, dividends stopping and dropping, and all values go down to zero. One wonders if one can weather one's own prolonged financial crisis. Iris has gone to Rhodean. We motored over from here the day before yesterday.

Iris, our elder daughter, at Rhodean became an example of evolutionary progress. I had been Captain of the 3rd XI and bowler (underhand), no mean bowler. My prowess was chronicled in the school magazine – 3 balls, 3 wickets. Iris played for the first XI and bowled overhand. As one reflects, however, I must add that her father's record for cricket was good. He played for Middlesex, Gentlemen V Players and captained Cambridge Varsity IX.

In Summer there were village matches.

Meyrick captained our village XI. Great fun, great excitement and generally whimsical wickets.

May 12, 1925

We have let Greyfriars for three, five or seven years. Tremendous packing up starting with sending Iris and Rhoda off to Rhodean.

When the younger children went to boarding school, we let Greyfriars and took a flat in Holland Park, London. It looked all right; bright, sunny, on the third floor with no lift, no porter, its stairs an invitation to any burglar.

I came in late one autumn evening. The front door was open, the lock broken inside, the flat ransacked, sideboard contents, drawers, everything turned out on the floor. In Rhoda's room a golf club lay across the bed. I thought she must have been clubbed to death, but I failed to find her, and she came home a few minutes later.

The second time we had burglars, I came in hot and tired about lunch time. It was a Saturday morning in July. When I put the key into the lock, the door would not open. Apparently, it was locked on the inside.

I collected a policeman and the door was forced. This time they had taken Meyrick's clothes, and among other things, a lovely aquamarine broach. I had left the daily woman in the flat that morning and in my own mind, I think her very tough looking husband took the stuff.

They are exceedingly successful, the burglars in London, and no trace is ever found of immense quantities of valuables they steal.

May 10, 1926. Braemar Mansions, London

Since writing the above we have found and settled in this flat. It is fairly all right and the only thing I could find without a premium and for 250 pounds per annum.

I am writing now because the Great Strike has been upon us for nearly a week. The organization of the Down Tool Movement has been magnificent and the conduct of the workers, quiet, calm, enduring and determined.

On the other side – hysteria – the whole paraphernalia of war in motion; Oxford and Cambridge called up; every man a Special Constable; regiments on the march; bombastic announcements from all Government Departments by the now entirely bombastic BBC says all loyal citizens must be on the war path to support the Government and down the workers. Already enough money has been spent to have reorganized the whole coal industry, which 'small matter' was the root of the whole trouble, as miners and owners agreed.

Locally, Meyrick is a Special Constable somewhere or other, and my nephew Puck, with a crowd of other undergraduates, regarding the whole matter as a huge jest in term time, is down at Battersea from 9 pm to 9 am.

May 11, 1926

Marvelous behavior of the workers. London is an armed camp.

Troops, tanks, guns, armored cars and every civilian a Social Constable and armed with bludgeons. Oxford and Cambridge undergraduates, however, are rather undermining the strike. Their Oxford bags and exuberant hilarity strike a universally frivolous note.

Alarm went off 4.30 am this morning and I had to get up and cook breakfast for Meyrick who, reporting at the Kensington Town Hall, was drafted to Gunnersbury from whence he proceeded to be a Special Constable. He was on a bus which plied between Gunnersbury and Camden Town and was called "La Grande Vitesse."

May 12, 1926

The strike is called off today at 1 pm, Special Constables must give up their jobs. Both sides have behaved magnificently.

Then there was the discomforting incident when I broke into my own flat. It happened that on Thursday before Good Friday Meyrick, Rhoda and Basil had clanked golf clubs and luggage into the Chrysler; my eldest daughter, Iris, and husband had arrived in their Bentley and loaded with clubs and additional golfers. 9 am they had zoomed off to the west. I returned to the flat to cope with spring cleaning.

On Easter Sunday, I woke late. The Sealyham, Choo, wanted to be let out, so I put on my dressing gown, took a cursory glance in the mirror, saw my face was greasy with the remnants of Elizabeth Aden's beneficence but thought, "no matter I shall see no one." Somnolently I went down the passage and opened the front door.

Then as I stood with Choo on the door mat, I reflected that I must go back for my latch key. At this instant a gust of wind blew against the door and it closed firmly behind me.

Gosh! What a dilemma! No way out and no way in.

Miserably I went down to the garden. There was no one about. London was steeped in silence. Returning up the stairs I stopped at the second floor flat and rang the bell; someone might possibly be in. Immediately the door was opened, and a horror-stricken expression came over the face of the man who surveyed me.

"Can I use your phone?" I asked.

"I'll call my wife" he replied nervously.

When she arrived, I explored my predicament. The man went up to look at the door.

He had great initiative and produced a long ladder and bag of tools. There was a glass aperture high above the door which let light into the flat and was in four small sections. He said he would remove one section and, as I was small, I would be able to squeeze through.

Foreseeing a gymnastic feat, I borrowed knickers from the wife. Everything went according to plan. The pane of glass was efficiently removed; I mounted the ladder and, while my ankles were securely held, I squeezed through the aperture turned upside down and headfirst, grasped the doorknob, turned and opened it and was hauled back.

My younger daughter, Rhoda, unfortunately had not taken to school life and was constantly changing schools. She was then at an educational establishment in Wimbledon and returned on Friday evening for the weekend.

I had given her the best bedroom. It had five windows, faced south and above it was a roof garden belonging to the occupants of the upstairs flat.

I met the boys who lived overhead, and they explained that in a tank on the roof garden they kept a cobra. They assured me that it could not get out and its venom had been removed, but it was a blood-curdling thought that if the cobra escaped it might come coiling down through the window and encircle Rhoda's throat as she slept.

Needless to say, husband Meyrick and I changed into that room, and thank goodness, four months later, cobra and boys left.

The next tenant looked above suspicion. It was some time after his arrival that my husband made his acquaintance and we went up one evening to meet him. He was a spider expert! In glass bottles and other receptacles of every kind, spiders lurked, alive and dead. Once again, my peace of mind was destroyed.

About 1927–1928. London

The following year the worst things happened.

One afternoon in late March I drove down to Wimbledon to fetch Rhoda. She was standing outside the school waiting for me. It was a lovely spring day.

When we returned to the flat Rhoda said she had a cold. I took her temperature – 103!! She had flu, and next morning an acute inflammation of the middle ear. The doctor punctured the ear drum and at the end of a very anxious ten days she seemed better.

The hospital nurse left. However, the slight discharge from the ear which should have dried up, continued and Rhoda had a temperature which went up night after night. There was pain over the mastoid region. One night when she stood on her feet, her balance seemed uncertain.

The doctors talked of operating. I called in another specialist to avert an operation. We worked hard with anti-inflammatory poultices, etc. and one night her temperature was normal.

Despite this when the doctors came next morning, they told me that they had decided to operate, and that the operation was to be that afternoon.

Our only hope was yet another specialist. I hoped, as her temperature was down, that he would veto the proposed operation, but he agreed, although it seemed to me that he did so halfheartedly.

So that afternoon, miserably Rhoda and I went to the Nursing home in Chester Street (London). Rhoda insisted I should sleep in her room. The operation took place. I stood outside the operating theater and heard the shattering din of steel breaking through Rhoda's bone. It was appalling.

I knelt outside and prayed. Eventually they carried Rhoda out. I glimpsed inside the theater. It seemed all blood.

That night as Rhoda regained consciousness, I heard her sobbing "Oh Mummy, poor Rhoda… a hammer and chisel….". And in the night, I saw a crimson stain spread on her head bandage. The nurse came and the hemorrhage was treated. Rhoda made a good recovery but all through that year I was anxious for her.

About 1929–1930. London

Priscilla had returned from a visit to Australia. She had been ill out there and had had an operation for appendicitis. Despite this, she looked lovely as ever. Puck, her son, was Aide de Camp to the Governor of Adelaide.

Puck was flying a lot; he had been the first to fly round Australia and now had decided to fly from Australia to England. This was before the flight of Amy Mollison. Priscilla hated the idea and was terribly anxious; in fact I think it was the anxiety about Puck and not her appendix that caused her illness.

One afternoon, the first week in January 1930, I had lunch with fiends and later was driving down Sloane Street on my way to Gunter's to buy cakes. As I pulled into the pavement, I noticed a boy selling papers. His placard read "Peer's heir killed flying." It couldn't be, I thought. It must be someone else. I gave the boy a penny.

"What is the name?"

"Grosvenor" he replied (Puck's family name).

I got into the car and drove back to Priscilla's house in Holland Park. The flat seemed full of people. They were anxious about me and how I had heard.

I went down to Southampton to see Priscilla. She had lost consciousness when she read the telegram. She now lay in bed utterly hopeless.

Before I left, I said to her "What shall I say to the children?" She replied, "Tell them Aunt Glad is dead. And so, it is. When sons are killed their mothers die – the glow of life turns to ashes.

Priscilla, who had been so gay and laughter-giving became the ghost of former self.

Puck was the eldest of the second generation of the Stalbridge's.

He seemed one of the most fortunate, had all the good in the world to make life worth living. The primrose path stretched before him and he was gay, guileless and unafraid. He took all the risks and could not be dissuaded.

He had wisdom, but like many other unassuming young men was reckless of the value of his young life. He had inherited the iron nerve and personal disregard for safety that his parents had consistently shown throughout the years. He rode his father's horses in the Grand National and won races for him. Then, catastrophically, he learnt to fly. He wrote to me from Australia at Christmas 1929, "Flying is safe, but my mother is terrified of flying." A few weeks later he was killed, the machine falling into the sea off Point Cook. Twenty-five years old, a tragedy of life unlived.

Unending sorrow, unending loss.

CHAPTER
TWELVE

Between the Wars, Husband Leaves,
Rhoda Married, WW II Revs Up
1935–39, Aged 56–60

"Life cannot go on without much forgetting this horrible century."

A t its beginning of this century, the South African Boer war was being fought. In addition to killed and wounded, thirty thousand men died of dysentery in Bloemfontein.

Twelve years later ignoring mistakes and miseries, out of the blue, came the horror of the Great War.

Those endless four years it seemed all young Englishmen were killed to the rhythm of an old men's' chorus, "Business as usual" and "you can't make an omelet without breaking eggs."

Then our nemesis; no leaders; no statesmen; the British politicians forcing a second world war and an old reprobate, Winston Churchill, throughout those years, showing the Victory sign.

Looking back most of the young men I had known had been killed in "this horrible century."

It has become almost the custom for young men to be killed, and the mind, satiated with terrible deaths. Its morality, its sense of justice lost. In the country today everything seems dilapidated, third rate, manpower gone, dead loss everywhere.

Charlotte's House, Greyfriars, in Tilford, Surrey

In 1931, we returned to Greyfriars. Two years later Rhoda married, Guy Lawrence, an armaments and airplane manufacturer.

Horror!

On this very same day, my husband left me and went to live permanently In London. Irrespective of personal feelings, he found domesticity irksome. Life eventually resumed its tranquility.

A wonderful girl, Margaret Elms, had come from Germany. She was very beautiful; her cooking was perfection and all her work thorough and efficient and seemingly effortless. The children came down from London for weekends bringing friends and hilarity. My poem for the times was:

I must contrive
To keep alive
All through 1935
For 1936 may be
The best year of eternity.

January 1, 1935

I feel nervous restarting a diary. I have kept one intermittently through the ages and now want to start again.

A disaster occurs and one has not the heart to write; values become nothing, and one has just to get through the day.

January 11, 1935. Greyfriars

Great boom on Stock Exchange. Good profits showing Marston Bricks and Tilling's. Priscilla let Basil drive her down for weekend. They only stayed one night.

This evening I attempted to fathom complexities of tax demands. Quite impossible! Those responsible for these tax tables produce a mystification as thick as the densest fog and make everything without end or beginning. They leave out essential dates and annually alter every possible figure so one cannot refer to the past, and finally sink and drown in a morass of ignorance, completely out of ones' depth.

January 24, 1935. Greyfriars

I returned last night from London. Rhoda drove me down and we brought down Claudius (later Snoop), a dachshund.

Snoop was given to Guy by Meyrick who, having had it for himself, learnt one lesson anyway, to look after a puppy is a full-time job. He simply couldn't do it and, by luck the puppy survived a precarious existence.

Rhoda and Guy are busy fixing a delightful house in London at Ivor Court. Everything new and spotless. It would be ghastly vandalism to allow Claudius to wreak everything, which he certainly would do.

I bought a lovely fur rug for him in Harrods yesterday and placed it in his basket. Today it has suffered pollution. Apparently, to save the time of walking him, he has been taught to function in his basket. The basket with my rug is now his toilet. Now, if the crass lunatic who taught Claudius this trick could have told Rhoda about this stupid idea, then my lovely fur rug would not have been ruined.

January 28, 1935. Greyfriars

The puppy has been seriously ill. The culminating horror being sickness during the night when the ingratiating little creature threw up on my bed.

February 17, 1937. *Greyfriars*

Awoke in Rhoda and Guy's room. I sleep there to keep in touch with Dawn and Nurse. Notice pines silhouetted against a fine day. Consider immediate condition – horror of the Spanish Civil War first and foremost.

Marie enters with coffee and rolls. Both excellent – the mail was deadly dull. The Automobile Association informs me that, despite excellent defense, I am fined 2 pounds for some sort of obstruction. I reflect on the day's activities, I really must do a certain amount of writing in this diary. I must make a determined effort and get out of bed.

I proceed to visit Dawn who looks lovely as usual and, thank goodness, in contrast to last year, well fed. I go downstairs in my dressing gown and let all the dogs (Choo, Nanky and Snoop) into their compound.

I visit the kitchen and instruct Antonia how to boil a chicken! I complete my clothing process and then, as Dawn is sleeping outside in the summer house, I collect Choo and Snoop into the house, leaving Nanky free to wander.

I go back to the kitchen and lifting lid of saucepan where a chicken is proceeding to boil, am shattered to find Antonia has thrown shallots complete with skin and roots into the stock. I make strong protest; remove fowl myself and replace with fresh water and vegetables. I collect vegetable basket and say I will bring vegetables for lunch.

On approaching, the neighborhood workman, Scutt, is digging up ground, and I am shattered to see Nanky and his old enemy the black retriever. I silently and fervently hope fight will be avoided. In another moment, the retriever has Nanky pinned to the ground. Scutt, vaults the wire, while I rush round through gate.

Scared by the united onslaught, and brick thrown by Scutt (this, I think, was the wrong method) retriever lets go, however not before he had bitten Nanky to the bone all round his ear.

Nanky refuses my condolences and wanders off into the heather. I go down towards the lake, where he joins me, and we return together. Nanky, thank goodness, goes into the compound where I lock him up and send for vet.

After lunch and my usual twenty minutes with Dawn. I spend considerable time trying to light my fire. Antonia asks me to see whether she has cleaned her room to my satisfaction.

I took the wireless man up to the roof this morning to repair the aerial and found it in a nasty mess. Dawn privileged me with another short interview after tea.

Mrs. Everett, the vet, arrived, and we struggled with Nanky, got him finally muzzled and bandaged, and she cleaned his various wounds. I have had my supper – beer and cheese – and the fire is now marvelous.

CHAPTER
THIRTEEN

Overture to War
1939, Aged 60

I have read that thousands of people fleeing from the rebels in Malaga during the Spanish Civil War are being butchered wholesale.

I feel as a Pacifist, "Why am I sitting by this fire," and grimly wonder how to secure the defeat of a government which has failed to get the Intervention Committee to function. But since the country has put a Conservative Government, as opposed to Labour, into power, they have the power to get things done. I can do nothing against the Government after all. I mean, really, Pacifists have not got the power to act and Government has. That is a definite fact!

In 1937, Basil was sent by his firm, Louis Dreyfus the trading company, to Basra. I knew Basra was unhealthy although friends and relatives assured me that it was all right.

I determined to see for myself. So at the end of July 1938, after Greyfriars was leased and dogs and cats and chickens suitably provided for, I started for Baghdad.

At Marseilles I was greeted by a Cooks' representative, who collected the luggage and myself and asked if I would mind another passenger sharing the fiacre (taxi).

The other passenger was a dark young man who could not speak English. I asked, "What is your language?" "Arabic, Madame" and so we spoke in French.

That morning I heard his view on the Palestine question. "The Arabs were warmhearted and hospitable; they welcomed the Jews to their country but would not allow the Jews to annex it."

At the docks a great collection of black troops herded into the bowels of the ship and these disembarked at Alexandria. The ship then sailed to the marvelous Bay of Beirut. Sapphire blue surrounded by the olive green of the Lebanon hills.

I stayed at the St. George Hotel built on the edge of the sea; balconies overhanging the water. The heat was excessive. The next morning, I descended to the beach. I swam to the raft a short distance out.

Arriving I found I had lost muscular agility and could not raise myself from the water. There was a Japanese man on the raft. "Turn around" he said, and, placing his hands under my elbows, he dexterously placed me on the raft.

Sitting in blazing sunshine, my eyes on the horizon, I saw a speck in the middle distance. A swimmer coming in at a great speed. A long distance, I thought. The swimmer came nearer and nearer, hoisted herself onto the raft and sat down beside me. She was a small girl with honey coloured hair in robust condition, not even breathless. She was German.

It was very pleasant sitting in the sunshine, and we talked about everything, the chance of fatal misunderstandings and the horror of war. I said, "When you go back to Germany, go and see the President of Women's Organizations." Tell her Englishwomen hate war as much as they do.

"Does Germany believe it's the wrongs of the Jews," I inquired.

"Yes," she admitted, "Yes, they gambled in our currency and Hitler will not forgive them."

The next part of the journey was severe, across the Syrian desert in Nairn's so-called air-conditioned bus. An awful experience. One is tossed backwards and forwards like a cork in a barrel.

In the middle of that desert, in the middle of the night, I got a severe attack of dysentery, probably caused by surfeit of figs at the St. George's Hotel.

I arrived in Baghdad, almost unconscious with pain and weakness and for a few days was prostrate at the Zia Hotel, the doctors decided I must leave Baghdad. The heat, in addition to other ills, prevented recovery. I was put on a plane and flown to Athens where a very clever doctor, an expert on dysentery, cured me.

At the hotel, however, the bills were exorbitant, and I decided I must try to get back to England. The orient Express seemed a slow method of travel, but we finally reached Paris a couple of days later.

In Athens, I had read French newspapers. It seemed; the French were in favour of yet another war!

The papers I had read in Basra, Baghdad and Damascus, gave the same impression; the public opinion of these teeming millions is in favour of war, "La Grande Bretagne must destroy Germany, a dictator country."

That morning in Paris, the French conductor came along to my carriage, he looked worried.

"They say the French Army is mobilized this morning."

"Surely not," I exclaimed.

"Times are bad," he said, "C'est au meme temp. C'est le meme enemy!"

Miserably I stood by the window. I had no strength to open it. A man standing in the corridor opened it for me, I told him what the conductor had said.

"No" he said, "It's s not so bad, only the reservists," and then he added, "I only just came back from a meeting about Peace."

"With George Lansbury," I queried.

Well low and behold, the great pacifist, George Lansbury, himself came along and shook hands with me.

I thought then, and I think now, that the frustration of that journey, illness, etc., was fully compensated by that meeting with George Lansbury, although I only spoke to him for a few minutes.

No one can forget the tension of the days and weeks that followed, and the relief in all normal hearts when Neville Chamberlain returned, after his second visit to Germany, with his guarantee of no war!

Then unexpected things happened, Chamberlain, instead of organizing a conference on the lines of the Van Zealand Report, announced in Parliament the necessity for maximum re-armament. The armaments programme already under way was speeded up.

Although desperately anxious by the trend of events, I was stupid. In my heart I felt war could not happen. Statesmen could not be so culpable, so irresponsible as to allow a second World War.

Surely, the power of my friends in the Labour Party must stand for the interests of the people; surely, they must stand for Peace. Then the political blunder of all time; the military guarantee to Poland.

Poland, which had everything to gain by an agreement with Germany for the very small price of the return of Danzig, the population of which was 95% German.

It seemed clear that Germany was not going to take orders from the British Government about affairs in Eastern Europe.

The British Government seemed determined to have another war. Unfortunately, no politician seemed to realize that Hitler was a militarist and would not take orders from the British Government about anything.

Weeks of palavering led up to this crisis – everyone is on tender hooks. Today Germany and Russia announced a non – aggression pact. Speaking personally the relief from tension caused me to be overjoyed.

This agreement was curiously reminiscent of the morning after the 1918 Armistice was declared and the First World War ended. It was difficult to realize then that the daily butchering of young men had actually come to an end. As I remember the morning of 11th November 1918, the weather was dull and grey at Westward Ho. I remember going for a walk over the cliffs the quiet hills with the murmuring sea with the sweet smell of gorse.

I had the same feeling of relief with this German-Russian agreement. I did not suspect this agreement was just a rouse and a prelude to another World War.

December 29, 1939

The greatest tragedy in the world had happened. Most of my friends are ready to reconcile themselves to yet another war. They have made themselves believe that war is a just war, a crusade of virtue to destroy Hitler. Anyone who does not fit into this scheme of things produces acute antagonism. What can one do?

It is impossible to read or be interested in anything outside the war and its terrible consequences. No one wants to talk to an old woman like me.

In days before 1939 when war did not look ominous, my old age appeared to be full of promise. I thought about the old days when I was young and my father alive. He had no radio, no telephone, no motor car. He died in 1903 before these things became a habit. Life in England in those days, for those with money, was spacious, slow, prosperous and comfortable.

The Peace Pledge Union (PPU) had groups near Greyfriars in Surrey and good meetings were organized urging a taboo on war. In those days there were great speakers about the stupidity of war: Dick Shepherd, George Lansbury, Middleton Murray, Max Plowman, Donald Soper, Bertrand Russell.

After 1939, it was deplorable that pro-war meetings had larger attendance. By then, people were being conditioned to war. There were scores of women in uniform. My experience is that most English women, except for mothers, are war minded.

In the aftermath of Great War, men were in a minority in Britain. By 1939, a new generation of boys had grown up. But in the twenty years since the war ended, the country still had a majority of two million women.

To these surplus women, war seemed like an expedient idea. It meant a better chance of male contact and romance.

War appreciation and patriotism of two million women is a factor in public opinion. But my kind of woman were of little political importance because we have few perceived qualifications to think, talk or give our opinions.

Mothers who should, by all rights, be given great credence are considered of no importance. It is essential that mothers unite to put a taboo on war.

George Bernard Shaw wrote that the only viable method to prevent war is the organization of conscientious objection. To me, it is a psychological mystery that in a world of peace-loving people why the great majority of individuals refuse to be pacifists.

Only twenty or thirty thousand people nationally have signed the pledge to renounce war and never support or sanction another war.

If only thirty million signed the pledge, England would have a major force with which to lead the world to peace.

I tried to influence my son to be a conscientious objector, but he was frivolous-minded and was influenced by conventional thinking. He had lived in Hamburg for two year with the objective of learning German. He had German and French roommates, good friends. All three had to go their separate ways to fight each other. Ridiculous!

He believed fundamentally, as I did, that the politicians must have learned their lesson after the dire mistake of the First World War. Ten million killed, every life wasted, nothing achieved except for the injustice of the Treaty of Versailles.

June 2, 1940

I took the bus down to Speakers' Corner at March Arch. Hyde Park was overflowing with people. There was a huge crowd around the anti-war platform. Fred Law was speaking very eloquently.

There were many attempts to heckle and interrupt. When he finished, he offered to answer questions.

Although I did not know it, I was mixed up in organized hostility. The pro-war crowd shouted a barrage of insults at Fred Law. I said to someone that the Peoples' Peace Party (PPU) stood for sanity.

Immediately some woman asked me, "Did I want to live under the German Government?" I replied that in my opinion no Government could be worse than our own.

The woman shouted out that I had said that I wanted to live under a German government. Then she appeared to go mad. She said she would smash my face in.

At this juncture two things appeared to happen simultaneously; Fred Law, recognizing me as the center of hostility, called out, with apparent disapproval "Mrs. Payne; please stop!".

At that moment Law was arrested. The section of the crowd where I was standing, cheered to indicate their satisfaction that he was silenced and arrested.

CHAPTER
FOURTEEN

Casualties of War, Cruelty to Children, Protesting WW II, and Basil's Wedding 1940–43, Aged 61–64

September 1940 Charlotte wrote her Essay about Cruelty to Children as the Casualties of War

October 1940

Yesterday as a gesture for mothers I walked round Marble Arch with the old banner I had used last winter, "Negotiate a Just Peace Now for the Sake of Children Everywhere."

I had a very quiet walk, no hostility. One woman said "yes, that is what we want."

I went to the Ministry of Information platform and received a good reception. The speaker read out the words, for which I thanked him.

On my way out, I was speaking to Webster, a nasty fellow who came up and asked me if I had been in prison.

"No" I said, and he wandered off hinting darkly that he was going to the police.

Meeting with George Bernard Shaw in October 1940

I succeeded in locating Bernard Shaw and took a letter down to him at his home in Welwyn, Hertfordshire. On the way I saw that the the bomb damage was universal.

Bernard Shaw said he would like to see me, so I went in.

An air raid was in process. Sun streaming into room, large fire, Persian rugs, chrysanthemums and lots of books. He said that he saw no end in sight. We had declared war on Germany. He said the press would not accept his letters. He had written to the Times and Daily Worker that week; neither letter would be published.

People who were not qualified should not be allowed to vote or govern. GBS came out and saw me off. I gave him a copy of the Daily Worker with its convention against the war.

October 23, 1940

I live a completely isolated existence. I am afraid I produce depression even on my own family who would rather I did not appear at Greyfriars to infuriate the conventional ones. They are doing everything they are told to by the press and the Government.

At the nearby guest house, where I have temporarily landed, I am regarded with great hostility because the fact has spread that I read the Daily Worker and thus must be a communist.

November 19, 1940. Pinewood, Tilford, Surrey

I was rather pleased to leave the hostility of the guest house and come to Mrs. Macleod's rather unhygienic cottage.

June 2, 1941. Chelsea, London

I am in a guest room in an apartment building before moving into small flat that I have taken for four weeks.

Last night when the sirens went off about midnight, I rushed down to the second floor (I am on the 5th) and sat on a hard floor with Snoop on a pillow till 3:30 am. That night there were no bombs on London. It seems the planes were going to Manchester.

June 22, 1941. Chelsea Cloisters

I have a nervous, unreliable heart.

June 25, 1941

"Hope deferred makes the heart sick in times of war."

I had a cardiac paroxysm this afternoon. I felt terribly hot and depressed. I felt like crying and, in fact, did weep like a baby.

I had lunch with my son, Basil at Gunter's Restaurant.

Later in the evening went to a mass women's meeting in Kingsway. I sat right at the back in the last row.

On the speakers' platform, there were about 6 women. Lady Astor, who raved about the virtues of women, as did Ellen Wilkinson. Beverley Baxter spoke on the courage of women and how they would make such a wonderful world after the war.

I managed to throw my voice successfully from the last row to the platform and asked, "Should women not act now and stop the entire war?" Which brought an immediate, enthusiastic response from the audience.

Beverley Baxter said smugly it was the German women who should be asked this question.

June 30, 1941. Chelsea Cloisters

Last Saturday two consequential events occurred.

In the morning at Harrods, I was waiting in the queue to get some rationed liver for my dog, Snoop. I spoke to a well to do woman standing in front of me who was in a fever of impatience.

I said something about the general and hopeless chaos of war, and it would be a good thing when peace returned.

"Peace" she echoed, "what a dreadful thing to say. I think you should know that it is dangerous to talk like that. You should be put into a concentration camp!"

I said one was still allowed to speak the Truth and "you must know that a conscientious objection to war is legal."

She said, "I have two sons in the army doing their bit to win the war."

I responded, "I have a son in the Navy, but I have done my best to make him a conscientious objector."

She said I should be ashamed to be a mother because "It is a glory for young men to fight and die for their country."

I said, "That sort of talk is neurotic nonsense."

Her husband appeared and she said to him loudly "This lady is a conscientious objector." He laughed like a hyena.

In the evening, taking Snoop for his last outing, I went around to the back of the tenement building. I thought there are so many children standing about that I would like to know if their mothers there feel as defeated as I do. Two mothers with two girls and two very nice-looking boys of about 5 and 6 were standing together as I passed.

They hailed Snoop as I passed. I said to one of the girl's mothers that it would be better to get these two boys out of London."

She answered shrilly, "I won't be parted from my children. No one shall separate them from me."

I said, "Of course not, but you ought to go with them."

Whereupon both young women, who had been drinking, shouted at me that, "They would not leave London. They could take it."

"What would happen to the war effort if all the mothers left."

They finally wound up the tirade by calling me a bloody old bitch.

"Against stupidity, the very gods, themselves contend in vain" a quote from Schiller.

July 13, 1941. North Devon

Staying with Priscilla who has insisted that I take a completely recumbent rest which means that I am given blanket baths by her staff. I hope two weeks of this will strengthen my heart, but I am inclined to think it has got out of gear.

November 6, 1941

Recumbent for four months in North Devon. The paroxysms almost completely stopped. In August, they had been so bad that I finally had to believe that my illness was the nerves of the brain ceasing to function.

Everything was ceasing to function, and my brain trouble was manifesting itself in an exasperated heart. Having come to this conclusion, I have been forced to give myself a mental blackout. This has been comparatively easy now because, thank God, Basil has been out of danger for the last four months.

It was no use even suggesting peace to a Government and people confident that Russia would defeat Germany and win the war for us.

June 4, 1942

Unfortunately, owing to heart disease, I am unable to speak at The Appeal to the Women's Parliament conference.

If I could attend, I would speak as a delegate from the Farnham Chapter of the Peace Pledge Union. However, there is the chance, with so many delegates attending, that I would not get the opportunity to speak. Which would be a great shame as I feel that my message is vital.

Instead I decided to distribute a handbill proclaiming the folly of war. I hope that this unorthodox method of claiming the attention of delegates will be effective and forgiven for its unconventionality.

Fully realizing the virtue of all points on the agenda of this session of Women's Parliament, I would additionally suggest that the efforts of all these women are necessary for peace.

Women's primary responsibility today is to save the lives of children everywhere. There is only one way to do this, and that is to attempt to end the war's appalling crime against humanity by peace discussions based on world fraternity and disarmament.

My handbill proclaims:

"Comrades! The women of Westminster have failed to stand for the interests of humanity. Let this Women's Parliament give the lead for peace by negotiation now!" *Signed C.E. Payne.*

August 1942. A Nursing Home, Queens Gate, London

I was transported here from Rhoda's flat where I had been invited for one night. During my visit, I came down with some form of 'flu microbe. I was laid flat for two weeks.

I think the fact that I had been four weeks staying in hotels existing on a starvation diet was the major cause of the flu.

During these weeks I did my best to protest the war, although my efforts seem to boil down to nothing.

I enjoyed selling "Peace News" at Marble Arch's Speakers Corner, which is a good place for observing the masses. During these visits, I received no opposition of any kind. People were very anxious to buy "Peace News."

October 22, 1942

I am spending practically all my time in bed depressed. My heart seems very odd and unaccountable.

I am trying to take less digitalis but can't get the hang of what is wrong. Thanks to my sister, Priscilla, I have had a marvelous opportunity for rest and comfort at her very comfortable house.

November 29, 1942

I have suffered a complete physical break down due to my weak heart. The doctor has ordered extra digitalis and not a foot out of bed.

December 9, 1942

One day last week Basil married a fellow Naval Officer, a WREN (no less!), Betty Cook, in Lowestoft, where Basil was based with his fleet of Motor Torpedo Boats.

*Basil and Betty,
both Navy officers, marry in 1942*

January 26, 1943. North Devon

A tragedy here at Curia, Priscilla's country house. A darling little green bird, Miss Harriet, died.

Priscilla had her for thirty years. She was a very clever little bird, almost human in understanding. She adored Priscilla. Miss Harriet really lived for the sound of her voice.

In fact, the bird ruled the roost at Curia and showed everyone that no liberties could be taken with her.

Priscilla went to London on Tuesday, January 18th and left the bird well. It is just possible that on Thursday, January 20th Miss Harriet might have got into a slight draft when the housekeeper cleaned out the cage. That night she had the beginning of diarrhea.

On Friday she looked poorly. On Saturday morning she was very ill, so I telephoned to poor Priscilla at 7:15 am.

Poor Priscilla in London had no sleep as there had been two raids. She came down on the next train and arrived here shortly after 4 pm. Miss Harriet was delighted to see her.

During Saturday night, Sunday and Monday, she made a great fight for life. Priscilla kept her warm and occasionally for a few minutes she seemed to revive and become cheerful.

But on Tuesday morning, Miss Harriet fell off her perch. Priscilla held her firmly in her hands to keep her warm until, with two little chirps, she died.

Priscilla, crouching on the floor in pink pajamas with her little green bird in her hands. Both looked very young – all the years seemed to pass away.

CHAPTER FIFTEEN

Wartime, Poverty and The End of World War II 1942–1945, Aged 63–69

May 12, 1945. 216, Sussex Gardens, London W2

Arrived at this nearly destroyed hostel two days ago. World War II in Europe was over, VE day, was on May 8, 1945.

They give one breakfast but nothing else which means one must spend the entire morning hunting for food.

All restaurants are filled by 12.30 pm.

Having failed to get into Prunier's, I went to Cafe Royal and had bad lunch of very tired cod and a mass of spinach completely unwashed, full of gravel.

It is impossible to get food now in London. You can only get synthetic stuff, pay an enormous price for it and it is not really food.

In these rooms I have a saucepan, kettle and gas ring.

My daughter Rhoda gave me six eggs and I am existing on them. Even a bottle of stout is unprocurable. Famine not a long way off, at least in London.

I met Clare Annesley at Marble Arch yesterday evening.

It had been a wet afternoon and was very cold, I tried to sell Peace News for her but obviously it has lost its appeal. I was not surprised.

Whitmonday 1945

In the afternoon I got slightly rattled. When I returned home, the latch key was not in my handbag. I hunted everywhere but was defeated. I wondered what on earth I should do. Then suddenly my keys were bang on top of my bag!

Later having a cup of Bovril for supper, I wished I had bought more than petit beurre biscuits. If only I had one suitable biscuit, I would eat some cheese.

I investigated my tin box which contained the petit beurre biscuits. I found a pound of some bought by me at Harrods last Thursday. There on top lay two water biscuits suitable for cheese.

Well, that was all very helpful.

At 10:45 pm, 1 went up to the lavatory to pay the last visit. The house completely silent.

I had the impression that every one of the lodgers were away for Whitsun weekend.

I sloshed the bolt across the door. Unfortunately, the top of the bolt rolled off and rolled across the floor.

It was a very old dilapidated outfit. I concluded that the brass top had broken off. It was very dark in passageway to the lavatory. It seemed I was trapped for the night being impossible to get out. This is a very old-fashioned house, lofty rooms with a steep staircase. The lavatory is on the second floor with two more floors above that.

Thinking the house empty except for the housekeeper in the basement, I thought I must make them hear me two floors down.

If they went to bed, my situation looked hopeless.

So, I put every ounce of energy into screaming for help.

"Help me please, Help Help!"

After about a couple of minutes I heard a male voice.

"Where are you?"

I explained "There is only one thing to do, break down the door. Otherwise I can't get out."

"How many are you there?" I asked.

"Three of us."

"Oh" I said thankfully, "Are you strong men? Can you do this?"

An American answered, "Why of course, it's easy to break down the door, so stand aside."

Then I heard a female voice during the banging.

"What is this dreadful noise? Stop it at once You must not break that door."

I lost my temper. "What the hell does the bloody door matter."

There was a grim silence and a male voice asked, "Can't you find the screw?"

I looked at the jammed, headless bolt, and said, "Quite impossible, I cannot even fix the screw anywhere; even if I was to be hung tomorrow, I couldn't do it"

"Alright then," said the American voice, "Then we will go ahead and break the door down."

Smash, bang and finally crash, the door burst open.

I was grateful but embarrassed. Four young men and a girl, an elderly woman in a peignoir and curlers were advancing up the stairs.

I said to the young man," Thank you very much indeed."

One of them in a crimson dressing gown asked me severely for the screw and showed me that I could have adjusted it myself, had I had not been so determined that the bolt had broken.

The elderly lady in peignoir, vaulting up the stairs, said that all the time she had been a housekeeper, including during the air raids, that she had never heard such a commotion.

It shows one cannot judge by appearances. All these tomb-like dilapidated houses were packed with people.

CHAPTER SIXTEEN

Charlotte End of World War II
1945–1948, Aged 67–69

October 3, 1945

Back in London. In charming, redecorated rooms let to me by land-lady of 216 Sussex Gardens.

Meanwhile the Americans dropped the atom bomb, by killing and injuring 250,000 Japanese, mostly women and children, ended the war.

I had my hair washed by Frances Fox, Stafford Street. I saw as I entered Bond Street a man selling paper like hot cakes.

I bought one. Japan surrenders unconditionally. So that was that. The end of the war, but not dreadful to know – the end of the killing.

Propaganda has been to exterminate the German nation. The Russians, having been given carte blanche by the Allies, are doing this.

Reason seems to have disappeared off the earth and the blackest of lies are taken as gospel Truth. Joyce is under sentence of death.

I visited the Freedom League today and suggested an appeal should be made to abolish death penalty. Norway, Sweden and Denmark have done this in their respective countries.

January 3, 1946

It is hideous the hounding down and extermination of those who can give evidence for Truth.

The Nuremburg Trial continues and the war criminals.

In England and USA cannot allow anyone of those men to live. It is a case of saving their own skins, but in all history has there ever been such a criminal aftermath to war?

To murder in cold blood your defeated enemy! They accuse these quite brave and gallant men, Hess and his flight to this country is an example of heroism, of mass murder. But naturally, every incident in war is mass murder.

Evershott Dorset, 1947

I am staying with Fergus at Aldershot in Dorset. Guy, his eldest son was killed in Burma April 1945. He was 30 years old and had been in India the last six years of his life.

He was very popular and had made a considerable reputation – integrity, reliability, horsemanship – fighting in Burma. He won the MC for outstanding bravery and then one day was killed by a grenade thrown in error by the British.

He was terribly wounded, a broken pelvis. He was flown to hospital in India and was operated on. He lived for two nights but Maude and Fergus have been unable to get information from anyone who was with him at the times or from the hospital.

Here is the anachronism, Maude and Fergus are heartbroken. To have a son like Guy, fine in every way, was a great achievement.

Now the harmony of life, the tranquility of old age is disrupted.

Maude, however, sticks firmly to her military standpoint. No sacrifice is too great for the defeat of Hitler and Churchill is her hero.

"He saved England." At the same time, she admits if her faith in a future life was not profound and all satisfying, she would commit suicide.

Explanatory Note by CMP. After WW II Charlotte wrote numerous essays about the futility of war, particularity about the misleading nature of wartime propaganda.

Daughter Rhoda's Story:
Protests and WW II

This is a WW II story told by Charlotte's Daughter Rhoda Lawrence about war and protest.

In 1943, my brother Basil was in the Navy serving in Motor Torpedo Boats. He was stationed in Brighton at that time. When he had time off, he would come up to London and take a taxi to Hyde Park where my mother would be parading with a banner on a pole with her friends from the Peace Pledge Union.

On the front of the banner was written, "For the Sake of Children, Stop this War!"

This protest was her occupation several days a week. At Easter, Basil visited. He searched all over for his Mother, only to hear that she was parading and protesting at Speakers' Corner in Hyde Park.

He took a taxi from Waterloo Station, all dressed up in his smart Navy uniform. When he found her, he would stop the taxi, leap out and greet her with great appreciation and love. He placed her in the taxi with the banner between them. They drove to my husband, Guy's flat in Sloane Street.

They were greeted by the housekeeper whom they both knew well. The housekeeper was meticulous and was continually rearranging and cleaning. Basil and my Mother would immediately go to the living room and have a drink.

When it was time for lunch Basil took his Mother to the Hyde Park Hotel for lunch. In the meantime, the housekeeper placed the banner in the drink's cupboard, propped up against the door. After a very good, and undoubtedly boozy lunch, Mother was tired. Basil took her back to her flat in Battersea, leaving the banner behind.

Later that night my husband, Guy, returned to his flat with several of the wartime manufacturer friends whom he asked to stop in for drinks.

Guy was the Managing Director of his family's building company, Walter Lawrence and Sons Limited. The company was an important arms manufacturer, which built Mosquitoes airplanes, as well as aerodrome runways, army barracks and war related facilities. All integral to the war effort.

When he opened the drinks cupboard door for his visitors, there was a crash as the "protest" banner fell out on the floor. The guests were very surprised. They assumed the banner was Guy's, who was deeply embarrassed.

Poor Guy had found life difficult for some time as he was unable to join any of the Services. All his friends had joined up. He felt unpatriotic. He would have loved to have gone with them to fight on the front lines.

Luckily for me, only the Home Guard would have him. As a respected executive he spent many hours on the roof of his office in Finsbury Square in the City watching for incoming bombers and directing the fire department to the sites where incendiary bombs had dropped. Roofs of buildings in the City of London were not terribly safe.

Fortunately for me he always came home safe and sound. Winning a war takes more than soldiers on the front line!

Grandson Meyrick's Story:
Charlotte's Husband; A Gentlemen and Scholar, but No Pacifist

CMP's Reminiscences of My Grandfather

Charlotte's husband, Meyrick, was well rounded and sensible fellow. A sophisticated man about town when Charlotte met him in 1906.

He played piano well, wrote poems, and told witty stories. He occasionally wrote and sketched for Punch magazine, the New Yorker of the day. He greatly admired the American wit, H.L. Mencken. He drew well and produced many pen and ink sketches, including the one of Greyfriars where Charlotte and Meyrick lived in the 1920s and up to the time he left the marriage in 1935. They were a good match intellectually and creatively.

Meyrick's passion was cricket as a wicket keeper and batsman. He played for Cambridge University, earning his "Blue," for all of his three years, He went on to play for Middlesex County and even for the snobbishly named "Gentlemen against the Players," being classy amateurs against paid professionals.

After marrying Charlotte, he worked for the Sudan Civil Service in Port Sudan on the Red Sea. Charlotte joined him there for a few short months. Grandfather's unkind and racist description of British colonial rule was "The Blues ruling the Blacks."

Grandfather Meyrick was no pacifist, Charlotte's major calling. Neither was he a war monger. In WW I, husband Meyrick served as a Captain (Later Lt. Colonel) in the Army, spending some time in France as a staff officer and some time in Cork, Ireland during "the troubles." As far as I know he was never involved in any anti IRA activity, even though Southern Ireland was a target of much German propaganda.

Between the wars, he worked for his father's company which had something to do with importing and processing grain. When that business failed, he went to work for Lever Brothers (now Unilever) in a division called Oils and Fats, which today would be known as Soaps and Buttery

Spread! The motto of this division was Lux et Vim, representing Lux toilet soap and Vim washing powder, but to wits like Grandfather, Light and Life.

In WW I he is said to have had the honorary rank of Brigadier within the Ministry of Food. This rank was bestowed to facilitate the Defense Production Act, not because he was soldiering. Still, he had war time responsibilities, which did not re-endear him to Charlotte.

Charlotte and Meyrick split, but never divorced, on the evening of daughter Rhoda's wedding in 1935. Charlotte never mentions him again in her diary. Anger aside, it seems odd never again to mention Meyrick with whom she had three children and, by then, a couple of grandchildren. She does casually remark that her husband was not interested in domesticity.

So, the question for the ages is why they split. Obviously, Charlottes' pacifist beliefs, bordering on obsession, were trying on both parties. Grandfather Meyrick liked witty repartee and good company, which by the mid-thirties may have been distancing for a pro-appeasement, anti-Churchill advocate. Charlotte often describes people who go along to get along as "conventional." She had little time for convention.

Granddaughter Belinda Milne's Story: Charlotte's Family

Charlotte (her family nickname was Lottie) was the eldest of four children. Her mother died on July 2, 1891, when she was only 12 years old. From then, Charlotte pretty well acted as "mother" to her siblings.

Her father was quite well off. He built a house called Seafield on the beach at Westward Ho, in North Devon. My parents, Iris and Ronnie Brooks often went there for weekends and golf. The Nixon family spent a lot of time there both as children (before the mother died) and as adults. Charlotte lived there for part of the WW II and wrote many of her essays there.

Meyrick and Lottie were married in November 1907 when she was 29 and he was only 22!!! Charlotte and her sister, Priscilla, were probably very naughty girls before they ever married.

Certainly, Charlotte was pregnant with my mother when she and Meyrick married. Soon afterwards, Meyrick went off to the Sudan to work, and Lottie was left alone in England. My Mum, Iris Winifred, was born on the 28 April 1908 and was christened in June that year. I am not sure whether Meyrick was in this country for either occasion!

By December 10, 1908, Charlotte is saying (her own words) that she ought to be nicer to Meyrick who writes her lovely letters from the Sudan while she finds it difficult to remember him!

In March 1909, Meyrick returnedd from the Sudan arriving at midnight. In her words "not the most tactful thing to do." In June 1909, Meyrick leaves again for the Sudan and she finds that she misses him very much!

In 1912, Charlotte ups and leaves for the Sudan to join Meyrick, leaving daughter Iris with Priscilla (Aunt Glad) and her young son, Puck, at Motcombe House with nannies.

Very little is said about Priscilla's (Aunt Glad to the family) marriage to Hughie (Lord) Stalbridge. Aunt Glad nearly died having Puck and never had another child. Both sisters had dodgy hearts. Nowadays they would not have been such invalids as they would either have had stents, or pacemakers, or even by-passes.

Hughie Stalbridge was the son of the 1st Baron Stalbridge. The baronetcy was created for Richard Grosvenor, Hughie' father, who was the second surviving son of the Marquess of Westminster. Richard's elder brother called Hugh also, became the Duke of Westminster. Aunt Glad and Hughie lived at Motcombe House until their marriage hit the rocks.

Charlotte's husband, Meyrick wrote the music and Charlotte and Priscilla staged a musical play at Motcombe which I can remember my mother talking about.

A poem, which purports to have been written in French, was, Charlotte thought, memorable:

If you would help me, when I die
Help me to forget to weep.
Let some most perfect music
Lull my sad heart to sleep.

Music will swiftly bring to me
Peace. And with failing breath
I'll pass from pain into a dream
And from a dream to death.

Meyrick wrote the loveliest music converting this poem into a beautiful song,

I do not know why Aunt Glad and Hughie broke up. I suspect the death of Puck in a flying accident in Australia was the final straw that broke the camel's back.

I think Hughie lost most of his money gambling, and owning racehorses, and the estate in Motcombe, Dorset had to go in order to give Aunt Glad some money to live on. Hughie ended up at Pound's Farm East Garston, near Newbury.

When he was dying, Aunt Glad went to Pound's Farm to care for him. When he finally died in 1949, she stayed on living there when she was not travelling. I used to go and stay with her in the school holidays with my beautiful pony, Chloe. I used to ride out on the gallops with the stable boys and girls, twice a day, once on my pony, and once on a beautiful racehorse called Red April who had won the Cheltenham Gold Cup!

So, back to Charlotte; in 1912 she went to join Meyrick in Sudan which she describes as "Hell on Earth." She freely admits that life was only tolerable with tinned food from Fortnum's and, at every opportunity, hock or claret cup or orange and ice laced with gin! She also played bridge, tennis, riding, sailing and sleeping.

At one point, Charlotte admits that "Meyrick alarms me. He says she is undermining his individuality. This is disastrous, especially as his individuality is charming!" For a while, at least, she loved him.

My mother, Iris, and father (Ronald) got married on June 27, 1928 at St. Paul's, Knightsbridge.

Charlotte bought Greyfriars in 1919 and lived there on and off, according to how well she was getting on with Meyrick and whether he was abroad. She rented Greyfriars to people because her three children were at boarding school. She preferred to be in London.

At the outbreak of World War II my father rented Greyfriars from Grandma who went to live with her sister Priscilla at her country house, Curia, in North Devon.

Charlotte's granddaughters, Dawn and Verity and Aunt Rhoda as well as Nanny Law were evacuated from London and came to live with us at Greyfriars. We all moved back to London in 1949 and Charlotte resumed living at Greyfriars until Rhoda persuaded her to sell and move to her house at Little Easton.

Meyrick and Charlotte's marriage was not made in Heaven. They married out of necessity. But I do know that Meyrick adored her. I once told him I hated her guts, or words to that effect, because she had done something extremely unfair to me. My word! He didn't half fly off the handle at me!!! He was very protective of her!

Nephew by Marriage, Anthony Denys Payne's Story: Charlotte's Husband, Meyrick Whitmore Payne; Their Family and Musical Collaboration

Grandfather Meyrick Whitmore Payne married Charlotte in 1907 when she was pregnant with their daughter, Iris. In 1908, he took a position with the Sudan Civil Service and moved, without family, to Port Sudan on the Red Sea, which was a crucial outpost for the British Empire because it controlled access to the Suez Canal.

After World War I, Meyrick was demobilized and joined his Fathers' corn brokerage business in the City of London. My Dad was ticked off by Meyrick for leaving the Sudan Civil Service so abruptly (probably to rejoin his wife Charlotte and their children in London) that, apart from promptly winding down the business, he joined Lever Brothers (now Unilever).

Grandfather Meyrick was one of three children of Arthur John Lynch Payne and Grace Emily Whitmore. His older brother (Anthony's father) was Denys Whitmore Payne and a fine painter. His younger sister was Brenda Tate (nee Payne), her husband was Major James Tate, commonly referred to as Tato. Tato was a great golfing buddy of Meyrick.

Love Song Lyrics by Charlotte and Music by Meyrick

Meyrick's Whitmore Family home in Gloucester

Many of the Whitmores and the Paynes were musical. Meyrick wrote the music for many songs for which Charlotte wrote the lyrics. In their most creative period, the 1920s and early 1930s, they collaborated well. Indeed, the duet "If you would help me" was a standard night club ballad, which Meyrick lovingly dedicated to Charlotte.

The Whitmore family lived in a lovely house in Lower Slaughter, Gloucester. The house is now rather a grand country hotel. The Whitmore occupancy dates to 1694 and includes some fascinating owners, including various Members of Parliament for Gloucestershire and Mary Wall Whitmore who was living in France during the revolution. Her diary recounts what it was like to be a foreign "aristocrat" during those troubled time. She survived!

On the Payne side of the family tree, many forebears lived in India as part of the British Raj, including Arthur James Payne, the Surgeon General of India. Also, by marriage were the Lynch Family, who unfortunately were somehow connected with the practice of lynching. How awful! But in those imperial days, lynching was a form of justice wielded by the priviledged.

On Charlotte Nixon's side of the family, her father married Susannah Evelyn Hampton who had an interesting heritage. Her sister Evelyn married a very famous Polish violinist Henryk Wieniawski about 1880. There is even today a Wieniawski Violin School and numerous concertos which are regularly performed.

Along the way, Wieniawski granddaughter Irene married Sir Aubrey Dean Paul (always known as "Strawberry"). They in turn had a naughty daughter Brenda, who purported to be an "actress." She was a society druggie. She became infamous for her socially unacceptable antics, including dancing on tabletops while under the influence. The story goes that she had her drugs, mainly morphine-based laudanum, transported by fishing smack into the small port of Appledore on the North Devon coast. She died in the 1950s.

With a family heritage like this, Charlotte was hardly a stranger to controversy!

Unity, A Collective Call for Peace

Abstract by CMP. Charlotte's condemnation of Churchill and British political leaders who seem to love war partly for patriotic reasons but also for capitalist benefit. Charlotte clearly shows her socialist leanings.

All people of goodwill In Britain today are in favour of Peace by negotiation now.

Against them are the warmongers led by Churchill, Halifax and Chamberlain, supported by the entire Press of the country, and the B.B.C. It is a powerful combination and very much in the limelight.

There is little difference today between Fascists, Communists and Pacifists in their great endeavor to stop this war. Their propaganda springs from the game source of Reason, Truth and Justice.

The Daily Worker, Peace News, New Leader and Action all write the same story and point to the same moral; the ineptitude of the British Government, the ferocity of the French Government, the well-deserved doom of the capitalist system and, a new World order based on World Disarmament and Free Trade.

This is a swiftly rising tide and should carry all before but, there are cross currents of infinite importance: sectional differences, political pride, prudes and obstructors.

When civilization is crashing, the rank and file have the right to expect that leaders will rise above party politics. Russia and Germany have set the example. They have combined but keep their respective political creeds.

It must be crystal clear to all of us that no political party can exceed the ineptitude and the criminal falsity of the Conservative and Labour parties.

In the supreme interests of humanity there must be unity between all men of goodwill and insistence on peace by negotiation. Men must rise above petty prejudice and party interest. The salvation of this generation is their responsibility.

And alas! For so many it is already so disastrously, too late.

Halifax and Henderson must refute their political errors and mistakes. If they insist on calling this war "A Youths' War"; then in all fairness, let Youth speak to Youth "above the battle."

A Fragment Toward Logic

Abstract by CMP. There is no logic to war because the price is too high to justify the perceived benefits. And the benefits are always magnified by propaganda which, to a great extent, is exaggerated by the military industrial complex. In turn the war profiteers get rich while poor people die.

The definition of logic, as we all know is in the "science of correct reasoning" and looking round the world today it seems that whatever other science may be in the ascendant, logic itself been put aside, neglected and forgotten.

It is non-existent in the British Empire and in the professed politics of Europe. Except for one or two of the smaller countries; Sweden for example, stands out as a model of cool, calm sanity.

The Europeans seem to have lost the power of correct reasoning. Russia, the hope and promise of Socialism, that theoretically ideal political creed, standing for the brotherhood of men and the freedom of the individual has denied these tenets.

Russia standing for Socialism has no right to murder her political logical alternative opponents – a sojourn of imprisonment would be the logical alternative to execution.

Russian propaganda would be improved if prefaced by the words of the

American constitution "we hold these truths to be self-evident that all men are created equal, that they are endowed by their Creator with unalienable rights, that among these are life, liberty and the pursuit of happiness." Although, to suit Russia's present programme, the last word might be altered, and industry substituted for happiness.

It is true that no country had incurred such universal opposition as Russia. The whole economic system of the world has been against her. She has suffered from external and internal hostility and intrigue. A panic complex has been created and panic action has followed, in negation to every principle of socialism.

The definition of Socialism must necessarily be "The Brotherhood of Men" and the code for this ruling "justice to the individual." The supreme injustice to the individual is war itself.

The philosopher journalist, Low, shows in one of his cartoons the hog and homo-sapiens and the hog says, "They kill me to eat, but you, poor sap, they kill for your own good." The irony of war!

All through history owing to the complete elimination of logic in affairs of state, men have eliminated each other. In the Great War, owing to process of elimination, the world lost ten million men killed, and was left finally with its politicians, curiously jubilant and congratulating themselves on the price they had paid for Peace. They doomed The Treaty of Versailles.

The Truth being that Europe was irrevocably ruined. The greatest crime in history had reached its fruition, victory. No moral values remained, only women, and a missing generation.

In the intervening years, events have followed their logical sequence and affairs in Europe have gone from bad to worse. Reactionary principles and injustice on every side. We have a new generation with us and still there is no sign of logic from those in power for their, and our own, salvation.

The League of Nations was inaugurated by President Wilson. Logically it should prevent war, but the covenant to defend each other's country, equally logically, blocked its progress.

The Americans, quicker on the uptake than the average Englishman, saw in collective security a "causa belli" and a repetition of the 1914 tragedy.

For, after all, collective security was the order in Europe in 1941 so they walked out of the League knowing that the U.S.A., for a variety of good reasons, would never stand for another embroilment in Europe.

However, they made the "Kellogg Pact." It was a gesture towards European peace and showed to whom it might concern that Americans remained logical. The League of Nations could not function for peace and at the same time include in its covenant that infamous clause for collective security.

National Governments cannot have it both ways. You cannot speak, as Lord Baldwin did, of the Fatherhood of God and the Brotherhood of Man and, at the same time, call the Socialists (whose political creed this happened to include a Bolshevik) dangerous "red" communists.

You cannot be a Christian and an imperialist. The Government cannot gain peace if paralyzed by prestige and arrogant nationalistic pride. It refuses to turn one stone to get it.

Hitler would lose a good portion of his moral strength if we had set right the remaining injustices of The Treaty of Versailles and considered the return of the German Colonies.

You cannot, as many have done in these post war years, stand for democracy and give your goodwill to Mussolini. You cannot stand for Peace and at the same time broadcast that war, under certain circumstances, can be the supreme virtue.

You cannot support the Kellogg Pact (which renounces war as a method of settling disputes) and support at the same time the Covenant of the League of Nations to come to the defense of all member countries.

It is time to study the science of correct reasoning. Man underrates the power of his own brain, the greatest of God's gifts to him. In his brain he has the power of knowledge, of goodwill, of justice and the supreme power to solve all difficulties and to find the right solution to every problem.

It is sacrilege to God to suggest a lesser way.

Truth, Rather than Propaganda about World War II

Abstract by CMP. For Charlotte war is a travesty but lack of Truth in propaganda is the ultimate sin because citizens, soldiers, recruits and citizens are misled into believing that war is good. Wars are started, waged and necessarily prolonged by the lack of Truth.

At this moment a great many inaccuracies are current which people believe are the Truth. They believe that Hitler wanted this war; that England did her utmost to maintain peace. They believe that Hitler had broken his word to England, and that England has been honest toward Germany. They believe that Czechoslovakia was taken over against the will of most of the people.

The answer to every one of these Statements is in the negative.

Hitler wanted peace; England made absolutely no move after Munich for Peace. On the contrary, she accentuated and sped up the armaments race, and with absolutely no pretense, told the people to prepare for war. Every form of propaganda was exercised to make the people war minded.

Profits in the armaments industry and in armaments shares have been continuous and progressive. Dividends of 25 per cent bonuses of 100 and 200 percent were distributed.

The prospect of war was popularized. Against this background of armament strength and public ill opinion, Chamberlain gave scant courtesy to Germany.

Possibly, he was overly sensitive to the campaign of hostility engendered by his Peace move at Munich. In addition to the fact that Germany had put an end to the buffer state which England and France relied on.

In their military part of Czechoslovakia was Austria, and that Austria had made many attempts to reunite with Germany before this date. Only the small country of Bohemia with its capital of Prague, belonged to the Czechs before 1915.

Nowadays to make an argument good people have the nerve to give no time limit to their national geographical adjustments.

I would suggest that it is permissible to remind them that the Northern Continent of America belonged to England 160 years ago, although we do not consider that we have a right to it now.

This war is being fought on the pretext of Poland. It's a determined effort on the part of Britain to reestablish in Europe the balance of power. For years the division of Danzig and East Prussia from Germany by the Polish Corridor has been an injustice. It was the last remaining wrong, in Europe, which was inflicted by the Versailles Treaty, upon Germany.

Early this year Germany approached Poland. She suggested no alteration of frontiers, but permission to make a motor road through the Polish Corridor and the return to Germany of the German City of Danzig with 95 per cent German population.

Poland refused this approach. Shortly afterwards, Chamberlain offered unqualified military support to Poland, and Poland renewed her determination to refuse German demands.

Cruelty to Children, Casualties of War

Abstract by CMP. As a mother of three and grandmother of nine, Charlotte consistently advocates for children, who are the first casualties of war. She argues that the damage done to children will impede the world's progress for years to come.

It is disastrously late for supporters of this war to voice that cruelty to children has incurred. The hideous variety of deaths which have befallen children in the bombing surpasses all known suffering.

Choked with rubble, suffocated, slowly burnt alive, bleeding to death and buried alive. Children have suffered all these things with the consent and approval of the British government and its supporters.

The alternative, Peace by Negotiation, which might have ended what George Bernard Shaw called the infernal crime of war, was rejected by public opinion, especially by women.

To remove children from the care of their mothers is a crime, both against mothers and children. The exuberance and enthusiasm expressed for looking after other women's children in the first months of the War was part of the general war hysteria.

Articles were written to show how much better off the children would be if free from parental control was propaganda and untrue. It will be impossible to compute the number of children who have died or been murdered as a direct result of this war.

The January 5 bomb casualties alone include ninety-four children under sixteen killed. This slaughter of children has been continuous over the period of the past five years; retaliation bombing being a matter of military expediency.

This is an irresponsible age of history and survival odds are against the children. You cannot put old heads on young shoulders and the children are too thoughtless to take adequate care of themselves. That is proved by the prewar figures of children killed on the roads and shows the fallacy and selfishness of modern educational methods which leave the children to look after themselves.

Peace should be the tranquility of order and there is time to put this thing right but when the chaos of war is substituted for peace the entire population of children is doomed.

I have grandchildren and they are tough, but the all-important sense of security is not with them, and when they have time to think, stark fear is in their hearts. Fear for their parents, fear for their animals, dogs, ponies etc., and fear for themselves.

I could not understand this summer why my grandchildren, Robert, Belinda, Johnny, Dawn, and Verity were firm in their refusal not to evacuate to the seaside in North Wales.

I spoke with them on a hot summer morning among the sultriness of pines. The atmosphere seemed charged with gloom, the children very serious and monosyllabic. Finally, they said they could not leave their pony and dog, which might be bombed if they were not there to take care of them.

The youngest grandson, Johnny, ten months old has been so terrified by the noise of explosion that he flinches at any sound, even the slight sound of a cough. The two little girls, Belinda and Dawn, eight and nine years old, held my hands very tight when I arrived and told me about what had happened the week before.

165

There was a colossal crater on the Village Green beyond their house. "We were under the stairs" they said, "and heard the bomber coming." "Now we're for it" they said. "We heard it over the house and then it crashed."

I wondered how I'd take it. Everything seemed so safe then, a sunny summer evening but, when the sirens went at night, the children cried in an agony of fear.

I remember an incident at the beginning of this war. It must have been in the winter of 1940, probably in December. I went to the Green Lines Omnibus Depot at Victoria, got on the bus and waited while it filled up prior to starting. Being early, I got a seat by the entrance door and watched the people coming in. I was feeling tired and jaded having had very little sleep. London at that time might well have been called the city of dreadful night alerts, gun fire and bombing seeming incessant.

The bus was almost full, when a child about nine years old stood on the entrance step. She was pretty and demure looking with wistful questioning blue eyes. Her hair was glossy and her skin firm and wholesome, she looked well-nourished and exceedingly serious. She was dressed very neatly in a dark blue suit and dark blue woolen cap. An unprepossessing rough type of man helped her into the bus. "Goodbye" he said, "you know what to do." "Yes," murmured the little girl and the man turned away.

The child, carrying her case, moved down the bus to the only vacant seat at the other end. The bus was in motion and I settled down to endure the trip. People got out, and people got in. It was dark when we arrived at Aldershot. The little girl passed me again and I noticed she had a label on her sleeve. Her destination apparently.

She was being sent just like a parcel. I looked out into the road. Surely there must be someone to meet her. She was so very young, so very sweet and vulnerable, but there was no one there.

The little girl stood hesitantly. The conductor standing beside her stooped down and read the label on her arm. "I don't think it can be very far, but I cannot tell you where it is" he said.

The girl looked even more serious and, as the bus moved away, started slowly walking in the opposite direction. "That child is too young to be alone," I said. The conductor shrugged. "We get them all the time now, evacuees, bombed out, their homes gone."

"Their parents," I questioned. "Probably gone too" he replied.

Today, reading the evidence of cruelty to children, I thought about that little girl. So sweet, so vulnerable, thrust into an inconceivable situation. It was obvious she had been well looked after and cared for before the politicians launched their pantomime of death.

Science and Politics 1939–1945 War

Abstract by CMP. Charlotte would often use as her muse, someone else's thoughts. In this response she emphasizes that even scientists, who know better, have embraced militarism and inadvertently promoted wartime propaganda. She pleads that scientists turn the corner and advocate arbitration instead of war.

Dear Sir or Madam,

Some years ago, one of the facts emphasized by the British Association at their Conference was that in a miraculous World the greatest of all miracles was the brain of mankind.

This affirmation gave me a sense of security for the future; that whatever the difficulties and tragic happenings the salvation of humanity would be achieved by the scientists who realizing their primary responsibility, would apply this miracle, this superpower, for the solution of all problems.

And now, civilization has crashed, and humanity seems bent upon its own destruction. Throughout the long agony of the war years, the scientists have made no attempt to save men from the results of their mistakes and follies. Science with complete knowledge of logic, philosophy, and relative values has failed to act. Science knowing that war itself is the supreme tyranny, and that Fascism, by comparison, should fade into insignificance.

Science, with its computation of cause and effect, knows that the death of ten million men in the Great War, has been the multiple causation of worldwide tragedy.

Missing generations of men mean ruination in the future.

It is outside the power of old men and a population of women to repair the damage. It would not make sense if they could. A better world through the medium of murdered men would be a blasphemy against God.

Scientists can demand a hearing. Science is international. The voice of science can be heard above the battle.

As Nurse Cavell said, "Patriotism is not enough."

Scientists by their silence, betray humanity. Consider what it means to the future, the same steps of causation will lead to the same effect again in the future if scientists fail to speak out.

No leaders, who tend to be primitive minded politicians, should allow the downfall of all civilized values. This occurs through apathy and lack of conscience for the people of the lands they govern. The speed and pressure of modern life allow little time for reflection.

England and Germany have only just replaced their youth decimated in World War I, a little more than twenty years ago. English and German children have only just had time to grow up. Unwisely, they trusted in their elders, perhaps because they had untrained minds, not yet capable of substantive analysis. Their confusion of thought was been devastating, helping to ruin their future.

The scientists bear great responsibility. Nothing less than the salvation of humanity is at stake today. I appeal to the Scientists of the world to use their analytical power right now.

Please, find a way to submit a basis for Peace by Negotiation so that the sensible people of the world can cease this folly.

Easter Sunday, The Irony of the Church's War Propaganda

Abstract by CMP. Charlotte rails against the Church which she sees as two faced. While paying lip service to God's commandments, the Church advocates for war. After the war, this dichotomy will surely lead to mistrust and skepticism.

A lovely day. Spring, soft and wonderful in the atmosphere. I listened on the radio to the broadcast of the service from Canterbury Cathedral. The sermon consisted of hate propaganda and a better world after victory.

In fact, in this sermon, if the estimates of military experts and politicians and the computations the losses of the Great War were considered, the death of ten million men and the devastation of Europe was advocated.

Death means nothing, of course, to Archbishops. They see in it a release from sin and an eternity of happiness. Therefore, logically to them, life is of little value except in its preparation for those millions of years of eternity.

In the Great War, a Catholic priest talking to me, and knowing that I was agnostic, said:

"If I believed as you do, I could not bear this war for one instant."

This reaction to war should be studied by those who have faith in orthodox religion.

The author Winwood Read, in his great work, "The Martyrdom of Man" argues that so long as men believe, confusedly or otherwise, in this future life espoused by the Church, there is no hope for them in this one.

This argument does not necessarily refute the Goodness of God, but it does highlight the irony of Church war propaganda. The belief in a future life makes man careless and irresponsible about the value of life on earth.

I very much doubt if Messrs. Chamberlain and Halifax would have dared to act as they did, had they thought: "One life, a little gleam of time, between two eternities, no second chance to us for evermore."

The horror of the Archbishop's sermon was upon me as I put the lead on my dachshund to take him to the park.

In the park the sun flooded down, the smooth water of the lake glittered and there were crocuses. I have never seen so many.

The grass had lost its character. It flamed, blinked and twinkled with crocuses. Thousands of them, mauve, purple, yellow and, under one tree, thousands, pure white. The crocuses made the world seem young, virginal and hopeful. On the water there were lots of boats. Young boys were roaming around. A girl standing by the stream. She was fair and pretty, and her eyes were questioning.

The Archbishop's sermon echoed over the water. His speech was remorseless and sinister. Suppose a steamroller drove relentlessly over the crocuses? They would lie, bruised, battered, dead. Such an act would be a crime: futile and senseless. But for now, the crocuses were safe. They represented Youth, Defenseless Youth. On the other hand, the Archbishop advocated the slaughter of Youth.

169

The anxiety and tension of these intervening years had wrecked most human hearts. My heart refuses to stand up to my weight, even though this happens to be of the lightest variety, and my dachshund on his rug in the corner of room, looks at me reproachfully and wonders I no longer take him for walks.

This Easter morning, I turned on the radio my bed to listen to the Archbishop of York. I felt, that, as on Good Friday the Archbishop of Canterbury had urged the English people to turn to God and repent. I thought that perhaps this sermon might contain some hope for a return to the teachings of Christ. Perhaps even some hope for Peace.

No, the sermon was confined to commemorating the Resurrection of Christ and life eternal. Not a word relevant to this disastrous conflict. Death was portrayed as the glorious entry to everlasting life.

The Archbishop preached that we need have no regrets for the millions of unlived lives, the young men, the grieving women, the orphaned children so damaged by this war.

Their happiness of the suffering was assured. They have entered the Kingdom of Heaven. Their reward was the beatitude of life everlasting.

The sermon from Canterbury three years ago, at the start of the war, seemed to have prepared the ground, made this sermon inevitable. The church has consistently espoused war propaganda.

War time sermons are the most powerful levers of war propaganda. Utterly irresponsible!

In this sermon, there was no mention of the irretrievable loss to the world of the unlived lives, the crime against nature and rue the will of God.

The Jews, perhaps sensibly, do not believe in the resurrection of Christ. They consider this belief the province of Christianity.

This war has given the Jews the opportunity to be consistent in their philosophy which conventionally is to save their fellow man from death and annihilation and to return good for evil. The supreme moral tragedy of the war that the Jews have not done this.

This 1943, Easter Sunday, after the service the bells rang out; they inadvertently celebrated the triumph of the warmongers Brenden Bracken and Winston Churchill.

CHAPTER
SEVENTEEN

Coming to America to Visit Basil and Betty
1948–49, Aged 69–70

May 21, 1948. Greyfriars to Southampton to catch Queen Elizabeth to New York.

V ery hot sun here today. Iris drove with me from Greyfriars to Southampton where she left me at the docks. She was not allowed to come near the ship. Queen Elizabeth towered gigantically above me. I had superior cabin on the sun deck. Everything is so colossal that all the passengers appear lost on the ship.

I had excellent dinner of delicious tomato soup, turkey and cranberries and delectable, creamy ice. My dining companions were mother and daughter from San Francisco and a man from Canada.

I telephoned my daughter Iris, who had gotten mixed up in motor accident. I had two iced orange drinks at bar, and then to bed.

May 22, 1948. On HMS Queen Elizabeth

Very quiet day on board. I made bad error. I had my deckchair moved from sundeck to be nearer my cabin which is at other end of ship. As a result, I failed to feel sun all day.

I went to cinema to see a movie called, "Miranda." It was too farfetched; Heroin was a mermaid. My daughter, Rhoda sent lovely flowers, lilies of the valley and pink carnations which make my cabin extra attractive. This evening telegram from Hughie, Priscilla's husband, very charming; also, a letter from Basil. I have found two cockroaches in my cabin. Spoiling to the sense of luxury. The voyage was sufficiently calm, that I was able to inspect the ship's kitchens.

The ship had a carnival cocktail party on the last night of the passage. That night I went to bed, everything packed for arrival in New York Harbor at 8 am.

I was shattered by booming of fog horns at midnight immediately outside my cabin. The noise was terrific, and I failed to go back to sleep. At 5 am, I got up and had a bath. The foghorn functioned every two minutes. The ship was at anchor. I went on deck; not a soul to be seen anywhere because the sea was so densely shrouded in fog.

We did not move till 6:30 pm when, in a blaze of sunset, the fog lifted. Then, I saw various other ships stranded at anchor. After dinner the emigration officers arrived from shore.

Basil rescued me from dense queue of thousands of disembarking passengers. He got me through customs with ease, even though I had no vaccination certificate.

May 30, 1948. Roslyn, Long Island, New York

The drive from docks to Basil and Betty's house revealed a marvelous blaze of lights. New York has stupendous glitter. On the road to Roslyn, there was a blaze of illumination and thousands of moving lights on the cars. The world all lit up. The solar system in comparison seems to have sunk into insignificance.

Basil's house is quite attractive, but the main road runs immediately outside and the roar of passing cars is incessant. Terrifically dangerous as all the cars are traveling at 50 to 60 miles an hour.

The next morning, we started for New York in Basil's Chevrolet. We stopped at his office at the United Nations which is temporarily in Lake Success on Long Island.

We went to big department store and I bought nylons. Basil bought deck chairs. The store was packed with every possible product. Everyone was anxious to serve customers and do any possible thing to help as it was in prewar England.

Quite obviously America has not really felt the impact of the wars. America's civilization has been one of continuous progress. Europe has been destroyed by wars and has gone backward by one hundred years.

Good food is abundant here, although the cooking not better than Paris in prewar times. It is wonderful to have delicious bread again and cream and every variety of cake as well sweets and fruit. The shops are open all day every day till 9 pm.

Last evening a very good-looking couple came for drinks. They discussed modern life. They described how my generation did not understand the necessity for careers, including business careers for women. They spoke of how my generation mistakenly believed that the mother should look after the home and the children. She was the chief director for publicity for Elizabeth Arden. Basil told me later that she was her husband's fourth wife and he was her third husband.

August 4, 1948. Roslyn, USA

I have had lovely weeks with Betty, Basil and children, Meyrick aged 4 and Antony aged 1. I have met scores of neighbors.

Weather has been very hot, and I have once or twice had a swim in a neighbour's pool. I have had plenty to read and lots to do.

Unfortunately, in the last few days I have felt very dizzy in the head. Seems like suffusion and poisoning of my brain. I have had a horrid sensation of tightening of heart muscles. I hope I will stave off a stroke and finality.

I was 70 on July 30. With my exhausted heart and having lived through wars, I feel finality is probably overdue. However, I do think that life is worth living in a world where war is taboo. Unless this taboo is achieved life is intolerable. Perhaps it is far better never to have been born.

August 8, 1949. Roslyn, USA

Thank Goodness, I have regained normality. I feel I must write down some words of wisdom.

Reading Gide's diary, "The Maxims of False Honour which have brought so many deaths among us" and "There is no fun in playing in a world in which everyone is cheating."

173

A quote from Review of Road to Survival: "Our ideas which evolved 20 centuries ago may be idiotic in an over peopled atomic age with much of the world in shambles."

Today is Sunday 12 afternoon. I drove with Basil to LaGuardia Airfield, where we went into huge rotunda crowded with humans about to be airborne. It seemed a scene Dante could have written in "The Condemned." Planes roared in and planes roared out.

Secretary General of the UN, Trygve Lie, who Basil had come to meet, arrived on time and was escorted to his Cadillac. We had orange juice and frankfurters at a bar and later drove home.

September 5, 1948

Basil has for the past few months been working for the United Nations recruiting observers to monitor a truce in Palestine.

This morning in Time magazine was the report by UN team exonerating the Egyptian Government of the murder of two French UN observers. They were presumably serving in that role as a result of Basil's endeavors. Both Arabs and Jews have refused to accept the UN offers to mediate the dispute. Apparently these two unfortunate Frenchmen were butchered by irregulars, when their plane, having already been shot at, had to land.

In August, I was ill having caught a cold from Basil and Betty. I was laid up in bed for five days.

Basil at the time had to get his UN contract signed. He made official flight to Amsterdam, Geneva, Brussels, London and back. He left on Tuesday morning, August 17, and returned the following Monday, August 23, quite an amazing distance in a single week. He returned at 5 am at LaGuardia on Monday morning.

Unfortunately, because flying terrifies me, everyone had lied to me about Basil's flight. They said he had gone to Texas and Carolina. I knew they were lying but not to that extent.

September 20, 1948. Roslyn, Long Island, New York

The Swedish peacemaker, Bernadotte, was assassinated on September 7 in Jerusalem.

Sometime this last summer Betty and I went to the UN in Lake Success on Long Island. We heard him put the problem of Palestine before the Security Council. This Jewish/Arab problem seems like a great tragedy for peace.

This morning out with Meyrick to the neighbor, Curtis's Beach. I wrenched my ankle and at present cannot walk.

September 27, 1948. Roslyn

This month, the tree-crickets and the Katydids, have been making the night vibrate like the E string on a fiddle. That is the perfect description of the stupendous orchestra every summer evening. The multitudinous insect population tuned in and fireflies everywhere.

By November everything will be silence. Then will come the long deep quiet until another spring; a quiet so intense that you can hear a snowflake falling in the night. The summer is over, and I am returning to England on October 1, just in three days' time.

October 2, 1948

Left Roslyn yesterday, it seems all the residents came in during afternoon to say goodbye. Every night last week we had farewell dinners given to me. The neighbours were all most sincerely friendly.

Basil drove me to New York. He, Betty and I had a very good lunch at the Restaurant Suisse. Afterwards, we put all my baggage into a taxi and drove across New York to HMS Queen Mary.

All my packages and luggage duly arrived in cabin on M Deck. I had a large and luxurious cabin. Basil provided whiskey and we consequently felt good.

Basil insisted that I remain in my cabin, as we said our goodbyes. Basil and Betty departed. He is a very kind son and sent me a telegram which I received with my breakfast this morning.

The sea is perfect calm all day with blazing sun. When I went out on deck for lifeboat drill, the man standing alongside me started to converse. He turned out to be Dr. Congdan, an author and one of the atomic bomb experts.

My foot was painful, so I saw the ship's doctor who strapped it up.

October 5, 1948. On HMS *Queen Mary* Mid-Atlantic

Reading the ship's bulletin seems like there are preparations for a Middle East war. Surely the Hiroshima bomb taught humans a lesson. It seems there is no possibility for more optimist news.

In fact, having read Huxley's "Apes and Essence," humans are supine and must consequently, perish.

That afternoon the sea was very rough. I lay in my deck chair most of the afternoon. The steward came with orders from the Captain to have all portholes closed.

October 6, 1948

We arrived in Cherbourg 7:53 pm. The next day at 4:00 pm we arrived in Southampton.

I had an agitating time collecting my luggage and parcels which I miraculously retrieved from the custom's shed and boarded the Pullman train to London.

My daughter met me at Waterloo Station among a seething crowd. We drove to Little Easton, where Rhoda and Guy live.

All in all, I had a very happy and satisfactory visit to USA. Thank God, all members of the family in order.

July 30, 1949

Last week down at my sister, Priscilla's house, Curia, I was terribly upset.

My red ring disappeared on the morning of my 71st birthday Waking up in the morning I had forgotten the date and went to bathe under the impression that it was July 29th.

The telephone rang. It was Priscilla wishing me many happy returns. The newsboy appeared at the door asking for payment.

I thought I would take Sammy (the dog) for a run in the field as the corn had been cut. The sharp stalks of the cut corn hurt his feet. He wanted to turn back, but I was obstinate and chased after him. I lifted him up and carried him for a bit before putting him down. I went to very end of the long field; the sun shining, a lovely day, and lay down on the ground.

I found the red ring was not on my finger; sheer horror because the ring was part of myself. It must have been left in my dressing gown pocket, I thought. I hurried back up the very steep hill. It was not in the pocket, nor apparently in my room.

Mrs. Wood, the housekeeper, had in the meantime tidied and swept with her usual efficiency but she is 75 and would not notice a ring.

That day I hunted all over my room and the field where I had taken that brief nap. The next day Pennington, the local farmer, came and hunted through the corn storks where I had lain. The loss was devastating.

Alas, the ring had left me. I had not taken enough care.

That last week, at my sister's country house, Curia, was overshadowed with a sense of loss. All that hunting and worrying, wrecked me.

I came up to London and stayed at Iris's flat. Rhoda came over on Sunday night. She saw me off at Victoria Station on the next morning at 9 am. I was on my way to visit yet again with Basil and Betty who had been assigned by the UN to monitor the Turkish/Greek dispute.

August 15, 1949. Shipboard in route to Greece

I left England on August 8 for Greece to go visit with Basil and his family near Athens.

CHAPTER
EIGHTEEN

Charlotte's Trip to Greece to Visit Basil and Betty
1949–1950, Aged 71–72

August 8, 1949

I left Victoria Station for Dover, from where I caught the ferry to Calais. I was on my way to Athens via Rome. The sun broiled down. I sat on deck chair crossing over to Calais, the boat was crowded.

Suddenly through microphone "Passengers Attention. There is strike in Paris, much of the transportation cancelled, including first class Wagon Lits attendants, etc. Local passenger train eighty-two will have places, first class cancelled and there will be no restaurant cars on train."

At Calais, there was complete chaos, no porters, no help. I got in to wrong part of train, arriving Gare de Nord as it was pouring with rain, fellow passengers advising me to go to Gare de Lyon to change. At Gare de Lyon chaos worse than at Calais.

After every attempt to procure information failed, a train came slowly in, marked on every carriage Rome – the people shoved baggage and clambered aboard as it slowed down. When I got on, every carriage appeared full but suddenly I came upon completely empty carriage and only noticed reserved labels when I had settled in.

On reflection, I tore off three labels. An English girl came along, threw her baggage on seat next to mine and said, "Please look after my stuff while I dash to have dinner. I assented and almost immediately and after her departure, a determined and vocal French family appeared in the doorway.

Seeing me and their reservations and name missing, there was crescendo of agitation working into a maelstrom of indignation, I must get out at once.

I said "No, not until Cooks man found me another place."

They looked menacing but I sat firm amidst the uproar. Unfortunately, when the young daughter asked me directly if I had moved labels, I lost head and unable to lie wholeheartedly, said "Je ne crois pas." Fortunately, the Cooks man materialized and found a seat for me. I asked the infuriated French to look after the English girl's luggage and then I stood looking out of compartment window for her.

Rhoda had provided me with two peaches, and the English girl contributed a banana and I had a few biscuits, so that was my supper. Every seat in carriage taken, six in all. A couple of crooks, moth-eaten and horrible people. The female, some skin disease on scalp, hair bald in patches, it was a most suffering sight. Every position impossible, my body ached, seemingly swollen and swelling in every part.

Severe brawls with the crooks on my insistence to keep one window open. However, at long last that leg of the trip ended, and we were at Modena.

The frontier police came and hauled out the male crook to be thoroughly inspected and de-clothed. Previously, I have seen him collect quantities of banknotes and stuff them into a pillow which he placed under his wife's head.

I found my trunk at the Douane and made my declaration, and porter, well tipped, said he would put it on train. The English girl had changed carriage. I had an excellent lunch in restaurant car. Very cool and clean, a great improvement into Italy from France, arriving in Rome 9:30 pm.

I found that trunk was not on train which was a despairing shock. Another English girl, Ann Cowdray, came with me to Hotel and we had orange drinks while telephoning and sending telegrams. There was no bath to my room, only a very stuffy one down passage. I managed to get clean about midnight and slept soundly.

My friends, Joan and Janina, appeared at 10:30 a.m. and we took taxi for a tour round Rome, Vatican City, St. Peter's, Castle of Borgia and Coliseum; all of which amazed me. Joan and Janina lunched with me at Hotel Eden. Thank heaven, my trunk had arrived. I slept all the afternoon.

Joan and Janina came back at 7 pm and took me to Hotel Flora where I left my luggage and I said goodbye to them there. But goodness, they appeared at Hotel 4:45 am on the next morning, having walked miles through pitch black streets.

At the Flora we got into bus and were driven to the airfield, where we had an excellent breakfast. The Italians make every attempt by good food gratis to give compensation for inconvenience and horror of air travel. The plane journey, thank God, was uneventful, having insured life for 25,000 pounds, I felt fortified.

There was some mist and we had to climb high out of it into clear atmosphere. Italy and France completely browned off – riverbeds and streams dry, not a drop of water. Greece even more sun baked than Italy and lovely Greek Islands and the Gulf of Corinth, everything set hard, rocky and barren in a sapphire sea.

Basil, a bit wind swept but very well, met me and we drove to Ekhali, a suburb of Athens high up on the hills. It is all very strange, no newspapers, no postman, no names to houses, but life is not completely negative, rather breathtaking views in fact.

Betty looking very well, and the boys completely bronzed. The little white house spacious, well shuttered and, sun baked garden full of fine trees, stunted and very green.

I arrived Thursday morning. Friday, an Australian UN observer came to lunch with his French wife. We all went to an evening party at UN residence in Athens. It was very pleasant on the roof, watching a brazen moon come up over the jagged mountain range and shine down on Athens which was all lit up.

Saturday, Sunday and Monday were holidays for Basil. He took us each day to lovely beaches and the water, being tepid, I swam. It is very necessary to swim as there is a water shortage and one can only have one hot bath per week.

On Sunday drove up to lovely beach, Canetti, on the road to Corinth. We inspected the Corinth Canal, looking down from stupendous, rocky heights to sapphire narrow steam miles below. After bathing in crystal clear water, unfortunately too stony for children, Basil thought we would try for a more suitable beach.

But, instead of inching along the coast, the road mounted and mounted, breath taking and precipitous and, as we could not possibly turn, had to go on to the top. The descent nerve wracking, only a fraction of an inch off the edge of a precipitous drop when passing another car.

August 19, 1949

Comparatively quiet life this week. Betty, having sacked most indiscreetly her Greek maid, has too much to cope with cooking and housework.

Last evening, I took Meyrick and Antony to a little pine garden in which a very small pond is situated. Meyrick had a fraction of wood which he enjoyed sailing around.

The pond had been emptied and was filling with fresh water. Some children appeared with a sack; they seemed over excited and were very noisy. A boy of about twelve carried the sack, out of which he produced a bird and flung it in pond. The bird looked very odd, its feathers had been pulled out and it was otherwise mutilated, its leg broken.

When they flung it on gravel, I went to protest to the boy. We could not understand each other, he only spoke Greek and looked at me with hard brown eyes expressionless in a sullen face. I then spoke to the servant person who was with them, but she only smiled blandly and with the two children there seemed nothing I could do about it.

The maimed bird continued to be tormented. I feel guilty but what else could I have done. I could not strangle the bird. It was a small duck, mutilated almost out of recognition of its species.

This morning, again at the pond where I took the children, I met an attractive Greek girl. She said Greek children are notoriously cruel. Meyrick slipped in the pond and I had to return to get him out of wet shorts. There were strong winds this morning and now it has rained heavily.

August 22, 1949

Betty drove me into Athens after siesta. We arrived about five went to the NAAFI – huge English military store, packed with soldiers' wives queuing for food.

They stand for hours waiting to be served and for goods to be packed and nobody seeming to mind. We went to an excellent, sweet store and bought Turkish delight and sugar almonds, all very expensive, but most delicious.

There is unlimited sugar here and unlimited sweets, perfect jam, and quantities of fruit. In every village and along the roadsides, mounds of melons, enormous melons of every kind, and unlimited supply of oranges, peaches and figs. Along the roads almost everywhere, acres of olive trees, figs, and vines, the smallest gapes, sultanas and currants.

So, the country, despite its poverty, has fundamental supply of food. But the poverty is all pervasive, roads appalling, rough, rocky, bad surfaces unrepaired, holes everywhere and far too narrow for motor traffic.

No pavements, pedestrians loitering and crossing seemingly somnolent, as well as few despairing dogs most getting run over. Transport archaic, except for the American cars and those belonging to the English and the very affluent Greeks, who, I imagine, are few.

The buses look thousands of years old, the trains don't run, and steamships intermittent and very few, in fact, everything a hundred years backward, the war having destroyed all possible progress and prosperity.

Paul Hoffman, American administrator of the Marshall Plan was in Greece this week. He congratulated the Greeks on their recent great military victory, said the war now over owing to their glorious efforts and that America was at hand with dollars to put the country into gear.

On Friday evening after NAAFI and sweet buying, we went to UN building, collected Basil and dined at a very good open-air restaurant, food and wine excellent.

On Saturday afternoon after early lunch and very brief siesta, Basil drove us to Sunion, it was about thirty-six miles, always surrounded by mountains which were blue and hazy in the heat. Alongside the road and covering the plateau, acres of olive trees, fig trees, and dwarf vines.

We drove straight on to the further mountains, over them and down to a sapphire sea, along the coastline and past occasional luxury villas, then climbing upwards the last two miles, arrived at Sunion.

Built on the extreme height of the cliff and almost at the edge of it is the Temple of Poseidon dedicated to Athena. At that great height it has a lovely pillared effect, but there are few pillars left intact. As such, the ruin is incomplete. Ever-lasting loveliness remains, far below, at the base of the cliffs, the glittering sapphire sea and the mountain horizon veiled in a haze of mists.

Sunion is the most southern point on the mainland and the Greeks built the temple as a gesture of gratitude for the sheer beauty that is Greece.

We came down from the heights and stopped at a little bathing beach. The water was tepid, the sea sparkled and glittered. At the end of the beach Greeks were pounding octopus pulp.

On Sunday, since the heavy rain last week, it is much cooler. We took bathing stuff and went again to Cavouri. We picnicked at the Taverna, having bought our own food and they supplied beer. Another lovely bathe.

The approach to Greece is through the straits of Taranto, the Ionian Sea, and the Gulf of Corinth. Athens is on the Aegean. Greece has a gem-like quality, set in her cluster of islands and sapphire seas and iridescent colours, shadows and lights on mountains, verdant green of pines and silvery grey of olive trees, sun glittering everywhere. This is the lasting loveliness, but the humans, alas!

For all the glory that was Greece, now poverty prevails and what can be done about that. It is a question of good housing, sanitation, and nourishment. The masses live in slums, dilapidated hovels, no sanitation, no clean water supply.

Yet out of the sun baked soil, composition of which is mostly stones and rock, they somehow manage to get a magnificent return in olives, currants, sultanas, raisins and every kind of fruit.

The population seem mediocre, average medium height, no superfluous flesh, thin, wiry and hard as nails.

Over two thousand years ago Greek civilization was at its zenith. Through years of history, there has been no such constellation of the great and wise as those who lived between 600–400 B.C. Their wisdom shines through the centuries, as the light of stars reaching us today.

Socrates, Plato, Aristotle, Pheidas, Epicurus: they gave direction and were listened to, unlike the deaf ear given wisdom today.

Philosophy does give the right knowledge of values. This knowledge is admitted as the chief aim of education. In their culture, the Greeks taught physical perfection and male physical perfection when seen is reminiscent of the Greek Gods.

I would set life to the teaching of Epicurus a voluminous writer, who wrote, about 600 books, but all of which have been destroyed. There is left his teaching by other philosophers and fragmentary words of wisdom.

The greatest of which is prudence. Therefore, prudence is a more precious thing even than philosophy. From prudence are sprung all other virtues. Prudence teaches us it is not possible to live pleasantly without living prudently and honorably.

Conversely, it is not possible to live justly, honorably and justly without living pleasantly.

"We therefore maintain that pleasure is the end."

"The beginning and the root of all good is the pleasure of the stomach; even wisdom and culture must be referred to this and the good life."

"A quiet mind in a healthy body."

I was never anxious to please the mob, for what pleased them I did not know, and what I did know was far removed from their comprehension."

"Live is unknown."

Epicurus taught and wrote against tide of public opinion. His doctrines were unpopular and possibly this accounts for destruction of his books. He wrote against faith in immortality, belief in creed and orthodoxy, against the superlative evil of war.

Disciples who listened in his Athenian garden may have been the first conscientious objectors.

In England today it is impossible to be epicurean, everything is third rate and synthetic. Epicureanism emphasizes nothing is good enough except the best, and the best is the simplest.

August 26, 1949

Basil drove me last evening to Athens and the Acropolis.

The sun was setting in tremendous splendor. We went up the steep incline past all marble, through the gate and climbed the many steps.

One does not see the Parthenon as one climbs. Other parts of the ruins block the view and then suddenly, high on its eminence, it comes into view. A great harmony of pillared perfection it glows warm colored with muted shades of rose and yellow, the effect of sun and time. Absolute beauty and a miracle of mathematical exactitude. It was built by Phidias to enshrine his statue of Athena in about 450 B.C.

We sat on the steps of one of the pillared aisles and watched the sun set behind the hills of Athens.

August 29, 1949

Yesterday was Sunday and we bathed at usual place Cavouri, but the water was very cold, summer has departed, very strong winds are blowing all the time and temperature autumnal.

Saturday after tea Basil said he would drive self, nurse and children to Parnis, which is a mountain 6,000 to 8,000 feet high. Time was limited as children had to have supper 6:30 pm and go to bed.

Consequently, considering the bad roads, all species of slow traffic, including donkey carts, cyclists, pedestrians, with no pavements. Basil drove too fast for my comfort.

The houses in the villages had doors directly on the street, we drove too fast. Dead dogs and cats are seen everywhere. No one cares. They are regarded as vermin owing to occasional rabies. Police scatter poison at intervals to kill them off.

At base of Parnis, one sees a precipitous zigzag track. We began the ascent. Terrible road surface, chiefly loose stones, after we had gone about half way up, there was a corner, with sufficient turning space, I thought notice was in Greek which we could not read, but at the bottom of the notice, in French "Attention Rue est dangereux!".

Basil seemed preoccupied, intent on grinding the Hillman car to the top. However shortly afterwards, what I had mentally anticipated happened, he realized it would take a long time to make it to the top. There was no chance of turning around.

He decided to turn around. I felt completely dithery, road space, comparatively narrow hillside faced with steep bank of loose stones. It was imperative to turn back. He had to put the car wheels on to stones to get additional inch of width. We moved forward to within 1 inch of perilous drop. Basil executed the maneuver and afterwards, inhaled nicotine ravenously.

September 2, 1949

After siesta and cup of tea yesterday, Basil drove self, Meyrick and Anthony to the Marathon Dam. Before we always drove towards Athens, this is the other way.

Mountainous country appalling road surface, sides of mountains barren and rocky. A six-mile drive and we arrived at gates of Park enclosure. The gates were barricaded with barbed wire and a sentry box and soldiers.

Chiefly through the exchange of cigarettes and Basil's indomitable insistence, we were allowed through. We drove down steep, narrow, zigzag road till finally we came to the lovely lake in a marble setting with pine trees thickly edging mountain sides. A marble reservoir encircled by mountains and the lake oblong and wide.

On the way home we deposited children with Betty and drove on through Athens to an outlying suburb. Cocktail party, British chiefly East Surrey regiment, and later had supper at a Taverna right on the edge of the Aegean Sea.

Tables set on rock ledges of cliff, very pleasant, perfect fried sole and orange liqueur, the water lapping beside us and shimmering in the moonlight.

September 3, 1949

It is a task of some magnitude to fix time chronologically between classical and prehistoric history.

I read that in Samos there are ruins of a prehistoric civilization, three million years old. The bronze age dates back 2,000 to 3,000 years BC.

The Mycenean civilization was 700 to 2,000 years BC. The Mycenean Acropolis and palace where Agamemnon functioned dates to 1,700 BC. His tomb is described as "the most remarkable monument remaining to us from the bronze age anywhere in the world. It may be that it was not tomb of Agamemnon, as it is alternatively called Treasury of Atreus."

September 6, 1949

Basil, Betty and I started on classical pilgrimage. We collected Major and Mrs. White from officers' club and started in the Hillman for Mycenae.

The road to Corinth along the coast is deadly hazardous, zigzag, blind corners, precipitous drop, heavy traffic, buses driving relentlessly, stupidly fast. I had my heart in my mouth, death imminent. As a result, the loveliness was wasted with such a lovely azure sky, mountains and sapphire sea.

We crossed bridge over Corinth canal from Attica to the Peloponnese over the dusty plain of Argos, to Corinth and its formidable Acropolis.

Roads leading to the villages flanked with Oleanders and Eucalyptus trees, everywhere olive trees, stunted vines, tobacco plants and tomatoes.

The harvest of tomatoes was incredible, stacked in the fields in huge baskets with perfect brilliantly red tomatoes. They had grown in sunbaked earth. After the plain we drove over hills and mountain, the wonderful scenery returned. We turned left off the main road drove about two miles and stopped at base of rocky hills.

Leaving the car, we climbed upwards through the Lion gates and into the Acropolis of Mycenae, great ruin of former splendor from 1700 BC. Agamemnon wrote about the "man of men" to describe the King who ruled there.

From this elevation, the view magnificent and panoramic, the world, its mountains and plains stretched for miles below us. We drove downhill to Treasure of Atreus. A miracle building, seemingly timeless in completion and architecture. A wide passage approach giving effect of lavish magnificence sides constructed of stupendous blocks of stone in a beehive structure of buildings made of same stupendous blocks. They are fixed circularly with mathematical precision up to the receding concave top of roof, no cement, one block placed on another for permanence This may be dated 2,000 B.C. although there is a possibility of error with the passing of thousands of years.

Basil, turning the car at these precipitous heights, we descended for lunch sitting under few scrubby pine trees at side of road, cold chicken, bread and butter and peaches.

Afterward we continued to Nauplia, stopping at a perfect sandy beach for wonderful swim. At Nauplia Basil parked the car and we crossed over in boat to unique island fortress turned now into hotel. It dates from Venetian occupation between the 16th and 18th century.

An affluent looking American couple crossed with us; hotel filled up with Americans. Three beds in each room. I shared room with Betty and Basil, cantilevered terraces where we had our meals. The food was adequate; everything seemed clean, with exception of the usual stinking lavatory.

Betty and Basil flopped into sea before breakfast on the Sunday morning and about 9:30 am. we drove back to Nauplia and started for Epidaurus.

The road bad surface took us through mountainous terrain, no traffic and very little sign of human habitation. I felt we were driving alone to the ends of the earth and then quite suddenly we were at Epidaurus, lots of people, seemingly all Greeks, very young.

Campers and buses and a museum, drinking fountain and celebrated theatre. This dates from the Dorian period, Greek luxury in 450 B.C. At that date it was Greek watering place with baths and a health resort. Asclepius was the all presiding genius, who initiated the system, He was regarded almost as a God.

The theatre, which held about 12,000 people is the most beautiful and best preserved in Greece. Basil and Tony White climbed the steps to highest elevation and could hear what we said when standing the middle of stage.

We returned for lunch to Taverna and bathed; same lovely beach as yesterday, it was all very pleasant, not a hitch, and everything went to plan.

September 6, 1949

Most annoying contretemps this morning, a UN jeep came to fetch Basil and, just before it stopped our front door, I heard howls of dog which had evidently been run over. I thought I would go along road and see what had happened.

Bill, the Greek boy came with me, at corner of this street we inquired at kiosk and they told us jeep had run over a dog. It was lying in road few yards away, thank goodness not the main road.

We went up to it, the dog was evidently in great pain and unable to move. I asked Bill to stay put and I came up here to Doctor's house. His wife Pauline came back with me to the dog. She and I brought to her house as she had a vacant room. I carried the dog back.

A healthy mongrel and very friendly. Unfortunately, when I moved the dog, it bit me very slightly, only a tooth prong. But this means that Betty and others are in a panic about rabies.

September 7, 1949

Thank goodness the dog has been placed. Its owners are away, their gardener came around and took it home this morning. The Greek doctor said he could find no break, although its front paw seemed badly twisted and useless. However, the dog much better than it was last night.

Betty and I went to see it after lunch, it has a lovely home and perfectly constructed heavy fencing all round garden. Had I not picked up that dog no one else would have touched it. The Greeks are terrified of dogs, owing to rabies in this country. The poor dog would have lain by the edge of road, either to be run over again or gone mad with thirst.

The Greek doctor urged me to have twenty-six inoculations against rabies. I said that the bite was very superficial, only one tooth dent. The doctor said that the slightest scratch could be fatal.

"Anyway "I said "At seventy-one I am probably immune"

"Wishful thinking" he replied, "And is the dog healthy?"

"You can never tell."

But I explained that my heart would not take twenty inoculations and I must take the chance. The rhythm of this place, Ekali, is all dogs and children.

My grandson, Meyrick, this morning went to play in garden of American friend. I took my other grandson, Antony, to the pond. On way there, I noticed a young man, very poverty stricken, he was carrying in his arms a puppy. He seemed entirely absorbed in the puppy. He stood hesitating, seemingly uncertain of his next move.

On our return from pond, I met a boy who lives opposite. In his arms was this same tiny black and white puppy. "Have you bought it?" I asked he answered, "No, we found it lying under a tree."

Finance in this country in state of chaos, which is a debacle of the capitalist system. American wealth feverishly supporting the tottering edifice but, unless American wealth has no limit, there is little chance of putting this country or those others destroyed by war back into gear.

There are rumors that the Marshall Plan and other philanthropic out-lays may break America herself.

Those in power, under respective leadership of Lloyd George in WW I and Churchill in WW II, not only gave away British investments overseas In this last war, to finance the underground movement in Greece, Britain gave away cash, gold, sovereigns and part of the British gold reserve.

Before the war, the pound was worth about 7 dollars, but today it seems the paper pound is worth the equivalent of 12 shillings.

War has caused prices to be exorbitant, 300 per cent above normal, wages minimal, everything official apparently a racket.

September 9, 1949 in the afternoon

We drove into Athens. We went to the Acropolis and inspected the ruins of the theatre of Dionysus. He seems to have understood "joie de vivre." He is said to have been a mystic. The evidence being that he declared drink, even in excess, a blessing. With drink, one left the earth and got nearer heaven. To be mystical apparently one must reach the state of alcoholic ecstasy!

September 12, 1949

We had a very hectic weekend. On Saturday the whole family drove out to lunch with officials, wife French and husband American. They live near Cavouri on the other side of Athens and about six miles out.

They gave us an exceedingly good lunch. Turkey baked in oven of local baker, every kind of condiment, cranberry jelly, etc., potatoes and salad on table.

Antony, Meyrick and two little girls lunched in small room at small table, adults collected the food and eat where they could find any place that could support a plate. The turkey was followed by excellent apple pastry.

After brief interlude we drove to neighboring beach to bathe. The usual lovely tepid water.

On our way home, we collected another UN worker Lucy, who was South African. Then we settled down to play bridge. I counted a suit incorrectly. I thought I had three winning tricks. I lost the rubber.

On Sunday, I was called with breakfast at 6 am and we were in Athens Hotel Bretagne by 8 am. Our party was collected, and we drove to Piraeus.

The King of Greece arrived almost same time, got into his motor launch and streaked away at 30 knots. Our transport fishing barge with a motor engine, was very safe and very slow. The sea was dead calm. We took four hours to reach Piraeus.

Piraeus, except for the narrow entrance to bay, seems completely landlocked. It was very white, very gay and I should say, a very dirty little town.

Yesterday a regatta was on, flags everywhere. The Tavernas were crowded, with the whole population apparently, walking in the street.

We had lunch under an awning at the edge of sea. A large fish and very unappetizing, fried potatoes were thrown at us. There were just too many people with no service. We numbered nine at our table; we ordered fish, which took over an hour to cook and cost 3 pounds. The others filled up with ouzo and consequently became indifferent to low standards.

Before lunch we anchored at small adjacent beach Basil and Greek naval officer who helped with the boat, dived off and swam toward shore. They found themselves in colony of sea urchins and swam quickly back.

Everyone else bathed including me. It was easy but getting out of the water seemed impossible until with some effort, I was able to fix my knee on ladder. I was hauled out by Basil.

Basil worried me by smoking those horrible State Express 555 cigarettes every minute of the day. It seems impossible to stop this slow suicide.

Our expedition gave us a great opportunity to see the islands. Egina is a large island. Our very slow boat must have taken two hours to pass it. Rocky, barren, precipitous cliff sides, a few isolated villages and a few houses scattered at some distance from villages. On the highest mountain peaks, there was usually a little church or monastery.

In August not a drop of water to be seen, all browned off and sunbaked, but one sees the water ways where waterfalls rush down when summer is over, and rain comes in buckets.

The sea had become quite rough on our return journey, the barge tossed and rolled ceaselessly; lemon juice-controlled abdomen for the first hours, but the last two I felt off colour, green throughout the rest of the trip.

September 16, 1949

On Tuesday, September 13, we drove to Athens to watch the tennis tournament. Basil went off to park the car, Betty and I stood at entrance to wait for him. At this instant the King arrived, very good looking and debonair.

It was interesting, the German player, Von Cramm, playing in doubles, unfortunately mixed. I had seen him last in Hamburg in 1933, I think, or possibly 1932, seventeen years ago.

Here he was playing with English girl against another German, Weiss, who had lost his arm at the battle of Stalingrad. For me at the change over, I thought about "the sorrow and disappointment that the years had left behind."

September 16, 1949

Betty and I motored into Athens. Betty called in at UN, I waited in car outside.

On opposite pavement fruit stalls, lavish display of fruit and lower down, bread. A splendid looking young man officiates here, well over six foot dressed in khaki; he totters on crutches with his right leg amputated. The waste is sickening.

Later Betty left me at a Museum, a great building with only four rooms to inspect and those very sparsely filled. A French guide with heavy cold in his head showed me round.

There was great evidence of advanced civilization in 500 to 700 B.C. Heads of lovely women with hair done beautifully divided down center and coiled on top or on neck, and well ear ringed. A bronze statue of Poseidon from 450 B.C., the perfection of the Greek God. The oracle of Delphi, also probably from 450 B.C. in bronze. This statue looks life like with crystal eyes and eyelashes inserted and wearing the usual Greek dress, caught up on shoulder, belted and falling in lovely folds to the ankles.

Possibly, I may have tried to memorize too hard, anyway at lunch in the officer's club, I experienced momentary brain cloud and poured tumbler of beer over table and myself.

September 18, 1949

Basil, children, nurse, me and Bill, the Greek boy, motored to Cavouri and in blazing sunshine had final bathe. After lunch on sands, clouds accumulated and, before we arrived home, a thunderstorm was in progress. It was a bad storm.

About 8:30 pm, I was resting in my room, when a colossal thunderclap and lightening dash obliterated the electric power in the house in pitch darkness, the children woke up terrified.

Fortunately, dinner was cooked, and we had it by candlelight, but next morning when we left am for Piraeus, power was still out, no telephone, radio or light. It was now time to go home.

After rather hectic struggle we boarded Italian steamer; most of passengers very second class. Food good, only little cockroaches, small species, all over boat, terrible stink in lavatories.

Basil and Betty played ceaseless bridge, I played evenings and stayed on deck all day. Went through Corinth Canal, saw lovely fox running along precipitous cliff side.

Complete calm of summer seas, Adriatic like a mirror, glassily lucid and clear; occasional school of porpoises, no other ships, the Adriatic seemed empty of traffic.

We left Piraeus Monday, 19th, stopped at Bari Wednesday morning for six hours. It was very slow boat arriving Venice Thursday afternoon, September 22.

Two days in Venice, or rather two nights, because we left early Saturday morning, on September 24. Betty and Basil via Dolomites, Zurich and Paris, and myself direct through to London.

Explanatory note by CMP. During the time Charlotte travelled to, lived with her son Basil's family in America and Greece, she wrote several essays summarizing the lessons she learned from surviving two world wars.

Why I am a Pacifist: Commentary on The South African War and Two World Wars

Abstract by CMP. Charlotte begins to reveal a religious streak in that man's folly war, fights against God's design. She advocates appeasement and arbitration as preferable. As such she becomes unpopular and even outcast. She labels colonialism and national pride as the unnecessary cause of the Boer, WW I and WW II as the direct result of colonialism and nationalism.

I am a Pacifist on the fundamentals of common sense and logic. Logic being the science of correct reasoning. War is hell. Peace is tranquility of order. There is little difficulty in this choice, and, in fact, it is only through falsehood and misrepresentation, that any excuse for war can be found.

To enumerate the reasons in favour of Peace would fill volumes, their names are legion, in fact every reason in the world is in favour of Peace, Pacifism and Appeasement. When you consider if any reason can be given in favour of war you enter the realms of stupidity.

Unfortunately, the English people are conventional, and they cover the consequent artificiality of their outlook by a great output of humour, not real wit, just broad, farcical, superficial humour.

If you are conventional the road is open for participation in every form of crime. You don't think for yourself, you lose all initiative, your values become unreal. Truth, goodness, beauty, those primary values emphasized by Professors Joad and Huxley are lost in the void of the conventional mind.

War is a convention and all those who support it must necessarily be conventional. World disarmament (we now know that present day man cannot be trusted with armaments of any kind) has become practical politics owing to the affirmation of the Atlantic Charter, by which every UN or League of Nations Member, commits to war to defend any other.

World disarmament, therefore, should bring the crazy structure of social convention down to earth; the only sacrifice entailed would be the loss of personal military kudos. The Palace of International Justice still stands at the Hague; the Kellogg Pact (to avoid war at all costs) remains word perfect for the security of Peace; the Disarmament programme of the Atlantic Charter can, by revision, incorporate all peoples. There has always been world fraternity in the hearts of men.

"When the pot boils the scum rises to the top."

Today the scum are given all protection and priority and they have the power of the wealth of the world for their support and, from every side we hear of the clamour of their bloodlust and rapine.

The war of 1914–1918 war was the ruin of modern civilization and, on a larger issue, has defeated the evolution of man or, in other words, has defeated the Will of God.

If an analysis of cause and effect were possible through the history of the world, it is my belief that all evil could be traced to the folly of war; progress held back time after time through the extermination of mankind.

When men give their consent and approval to the bombing of women and children, we realize that human degradation is complete and that we have gone back to the extreme limits of barbarism.

I am a Pacifist on the fundamentals of common sense and logic. This is true but when war, in its horror and injustice, descends on the people. Then they are trapped through no fault of their own by irresponsible leaders in this policy of universal death.

One lives in a lunatic world where common sense and logic have no place, and, as woman and a mother, one fights with every fraction of energy for Truth, and against the vile wastage of unlived lives; against the ruin of the world for future generations; against the crimes of self-righteous of primitive minded politicians; against the ferocity and fatuity of feminine ignorance and one fights for the return of reason, sanity, and for the life of one's own son and the life of every other mother's son.

Owing to the power of lies and propaganda, together with the credulity and apathy of the people, the fight is a losing one.

The same evil powers that frustrate and defeat the mothers, defeat also the man in the street; his heart in all probability craves for just that one order, the TRANQUILITY OF PEACE.

The answer is plain, the man in the street must speak the Truth about himself and proclaim himself for all time a Pacifist.

Looking back the justification for Pacifism is tragically proved. I remember the happiness of life before the South African war, the consciousness of the security of our civilization. Penny postage stamps, income tax practically nil, Britain exceedingly prosperous, a flow of gold from South Africa and a new genius cropping up, personified by the South African millionaire.

Suddenly, voiced in the press and swelling into a clamour, the wrongs of the South African Uitlanders.

My first consciousness of pacifism was the feeling of outrage experienced when, in answer to the President of South Africa Kruger's reasoned protest to the British Government, the latter replied in a bombastic tone which was practically a declaration of war. At that time, I found myself generally in a minority of one and labelled pro-Boer.

The excuse given for the crime of the Boer War was prestige – British prestige. Thousands of young men were killed or died of typhoid, their lives wasted, and history declared the war a mistake. The recuperative power of humanity is founded on its failure to remember.

The continuous flow of gold from South Africa contributed towards England's prosperity; everyone seemed rich and contented. The reality was an abundance of wealth for everyone and Lloyd George was making a great endeavor for the poverty-stricken masses and a fair distribution of wealth.

Everything seemed set for happiness and construction in the best of all possible worlds.

Then suddenly, out of the blue, smashing all hope in civilization, the First World War. In this war the people were deafened and duped by the clamour of lies and propaganda.

I believed what the newspapers told us in the first six months of that war; that Germany was responsible, and that the Kaiser was the incarnation of evil.

Later the Truth emerged, and Austria and Russia were labelled with primary responsibility but that was years afterwards. Only then, did scholars begin to write books about it.

In 1915, the Women's International League was founded. Its object, Peace by Negotiation to end the war. I expected all women would join and support this, but to my amazement I began to realize the unbelievable. Women said they did not want Peace.

Nothing one could say would bring them to understand the meaning of war. Even if they believed the lies of the press about war, it seemed to me incredible that they should not do all in their power to stop the monstrous injustice of young men being killed and being forced to kill each other. A death-trap set by the folly of politicians.

From the Continent came various attempts for peace. Quoting from my diary, December 18, 1915, "In the Reichstag December 10th, German Chancellor suggests Peace on the basis: no annexation by conquest and guarantees for Germany's safety.

But if I ask, why this should not be considered, this Peace attempt, I am called pro-German and traitor.

"We are fighting, they say, for a better world for the children, to prevent the Germans being able to do this a second time, to give us peace for the next hundred years."

The British Government refused to consider Peace by negotiation. Ten million men were killed to consummate the Treaty of Versailles, and its direct consequence, the Second World war.

McGovern, speaking at the Leaders for Peace Conference in April 1943, said "This war has gone on for over three and a half years. Over ten million men, women and children have died by military action and bombing, or persecution and disease; millions more have been disabled and left as physical wrecks."

Over twenty million people killed by military action in the last three decades! This is the incredible disgrace of our civilization and the indictment against war.

Pacifism must necessarily be the political code of the future. It is the only practical politics: World Fraternity and World Disarmament.

War through the ages has proved itself the suicide of humanity. To what heights of Goodness, Truth, and Beauty could man have risen had it not been for the defeatism of war.

Pantomime, The Folly of the Second World War 1939–1945

Abstract by CMP. Charlotte raged against war time propaganda, which she considered the Devil's work, leading people into stupid battles. Throughout her diary she spells Truth with a capital T as she regards Truth as a message which motivates warlike behavior. She calls the lies and war time cheer as a pantomime, which creates a sense of unreality. People cheer when young men die.

There must be no explanation. Everyone dumb, completely dumb, and with that one can get away with anything.

"Lift up your hearts and smile." These are the directions from the warmonger, Brendan Bracken and the BBC.

Raucous laughter, worker's playtime, puerile jokes. Careless talk costs lives, so not one word. Truth and reason swept outside the war area and the war area is the world. Total war.

The devil has come into his own. Hell, on earth. His voice the loudspeakers to the world.

Oxford accent, smug, complacent; everything one reads, books, the press, under his control. The Government also, the yes men are there, there to do his bidding.

A holocaust of death and no thought. Everything camouflaged, vice posing as virtue. Lies, glittering lies.

The prime minister, Winston Churchill, sending his country to perdition, glorified as it's savior. A great chorus and company mouthing war appreciation. Church dignitaries pointing to Heaven – apparently a reward for virtue and murder most foul.

And women in the pantomime many of them have turned into geese, their cackle rises above the turmoil.

Everyone in lock step. We'll call it "Uniform," chortled the Devil, naming his pantomime. All on one pattern. Minds and bodies in uniform. And there it was the orgy of unreason.

Minds drugged with drink and nicotine and nonstop energy; everyone kept on the move ceaselessly.

Hell, on earth. Destruction rained from the skies. Human habitations, traditions, their towns, homes, happiness, children, dependent friends, dogs, cats, birds, all civilized virtues, burning together in fierce conflagration: nothing left.

An incredible, inconceivable crime backed by uniform consent. Stupendous tragedy! All an historical record of torture, torment, massacre, insignificant by comparison, and this in the name of virtue and to enforce God's pattern of the world.

But on with the pantomime. A meaningless uproar. A welter of evil. All good intentions – all goodness and youth, trusting, guileless youth, knocked out of the way.

Killed stone dead. Life defeated, possibly for centuries. And with youth, tradition, goodwill, innocence, all this trampled into the mire, into the filth into the great rivers of blood, a rising tide which flows swiftly behind the make-believe scenery.

In the finale to this horrible war, a chorus of justification. It is the birth year of the holocaust (Holy Crusade) launched by neurotics in the name of freedom. The devastation of Europe, in the name of liberation is complete.

In the foreground of the pantomime are the death-pits of isolation and concentration camps.

The war-makers themselves responsible for the wreaking of civilization and all civilized values, for the concept and prolongation of the war and chaos, the consequent death and torment of millions of human beings, I weep for the victims of disease and famine.

Whipped into a frenzy of self-righteousness by the crazy rhythm of the Devil's orchestra – they howl their nauseating hypocrisy. The Devil laughs. His triumph is complete. In the orchestra, the drums of death beat continuously, non-stop, but the pantomime must end. It is the time for the harlequinade.

The Second World War officially ended in Europe on May 4, 1945.

Confusion of Thought, About the Lessons of World War II

Abstract by CMP. In this essay, Charlotte approaches the concept of a "just war." However, she continues to advocate arbitration and appeasement because, although justified there are no winners and the sooner war is over, the better.

War itself spells confusion, and every moment of its duration this confusion becomes greater. People lose their sense of right values. The life of the individual counts for nothing.

Lives and wealth are squandered for the abstract thing, notions of national honour and national pride.

Nature is outraged and, in the appalling confusion of thought, people strive to find some excuse for it all, some compensation for sacrifice. Fatalists declare it had to be.

Egotists say, "We deserved it and, taking it as a war of retribution, affirm that it will raise the morale of the individual. Other people, unintentionally sacrilegious, call it, "The Will of God."

I would revise the allegory of Adam and Eve. God gave man the world, "The Garden Eden." He gave him also the knowledge of right and wrong.

Man spoiled the garden then and continues to do so now by war. War is devastation, it arrests progress and wastes all that progress has accomplished.

Civilization has been thrown back time after time, by war and nations have perished in the aftermath of war: exhaustion.

Arnold Bennett wrote the other day, "This murder and crippling of males, which for conscience sake, we call war."

Dr Saleeby, the proponent of eugenics, shows that from the eugenic point of view, racial degeneration is the direct effect of war.

Roosevelt's book, "Why America Should Join the Allies" is prefaced by the remark of an American soldier, General Sherman, "War is Hell." He was right.

Thoughtful men all over the world are unanimous in the opinion that war is wholly bad.

Austria, the Kaiser and his people, have thought otherwise and destroyed Europe. Serbia, Belgium, and a large part of Poland are devastated and ruined, and the world is the loser of hundreds of thousands of men and boys who have sacrificed their birthright and suffered unspeakable pain and horror.

Women, the women who have lost all that made life worth living are as the dead ashes of themselves.

Yet in the face of these facts, confusion of thought still prevails.

Some people are deficient in knowledge, others are deficient in imagination, and some are densely stupid. Their influence is pernicious. They call black, white and misconstrue the meaning of words. They are everywhere, these people; one meets them and dreads their jarring clamour in the press. To them war is not wholly bad. The agony, blood, sweat and crucifixion of the individual, these words are too strong.

"He fell on the field of battle" is a better phrase and less descriptive.

The word, international reduces them to a hysteria of fury. To the foolish, international means pro-German.

They cannot understand that my admiration for England and Englishmen, and for what the Allies have done and are still doing, is consistent with one's detestation of war.

Daily casualty lists have a demoralizing effect. The realization of what they mean is a torture which, possibly, it is best to spare oneself.

People avoid the realization and the dead men appear as so many numbers on the colossal stake of war.

There is a definition of Carlyle's which shows what death means to the individual, "One life: a little gleam of time between two eternities, no second chance to us for evermore."

We know that England, France and Russia did not want war, their intentions towards Germany and Austria had been obviously pacifist like.

When Austria attacked Serbia and the Germans attacked Belgium the allies had to fight.

There was no of alternative. The Allies are fighting in the cause of Justice and Civilization, but the evils of war are not thereby lessened for them.

To gloss over and minimize these evils is the trend of today's thought and it seems almost as sinful as that hideous travesty, "Business as usual."

"Business as usual" when civilization is over-thrown, and the world's greatest tragedy is under way. Speculation is rife as to the after effect of war.

Hopefully, owing to the magnitude of this disaster and its appalling consequences, men will see to it that it does not occur again. Pray that war in the future may be averted and peace be assured; but, in no way, does this hope and prayer correct the evils of this war.

The culminating evil, the colossal loss of male lives, the total of which, when history is written, will surely "stagger humanity." Nature arranges for an even balance of the sexes and one cannot outrage nature with impunity.

The result to thousands of women, who should have been wives and mothers, must be productive of ill will, evil and degeneration. In fact, the direct and indirect evils resulting from the fighting nations is incalculable.

The world is not over-populated. The survival of the fittest is not ensured by artillery duels. Man is not necessarily decadent or cowardly because he has no lust for blood.

Germany has nurtured a chimera of world enrichment through power and expansion of trade through war. Have the results of the past months taught Germany the lesson of "the Great Illusion"? Who knows, but that is not likely as mankind will continue to be confused and stupidly praise the need for war.

Women: After the Wars and Now

Abstract by CMP. Charlotte is severely pained by the reaction of women to war, she argues that women, who become wives and mothers, should know better as it is they who lose boyfriends, husbands, sons and daughters. In this essay she is responding to an op-ed which suggested women should support the war effort.

Several most misleading articles have been written on this subject. One by author Twells Brex, who wrote the 1923 novel, Conqueror of Death, which prattles on about woman' s place after the war. I disagree.

Women have had their place in the sun in America and they are still there.

They have time and leisure to watch and understand the horror of what is happening in Europe.

Only in the last hundred years has the world become, humanly speaking, civilized. The power of steam, machinery, the potential of an inexpensive newspapers, the whole scheme of mechanical force have revolutionized the world.

Although in proportion to the population, the dregs of humanity have multiplied. Yet the whole trend of civilization and consequent education has been towards a higher morality and justice.

A hundred years ago, England stood at the head of civilized community yet, in her scheme of justice, children suffered capital punishment for stealing. Among the various discrepancies of thought at the present time is the idea that wars have not historically hurt or demoralized England.

England has never experienced the wholesale slaughter of her youth but the past two wars, probably in the direct line of cause and effect, account for the fact that she was barely civilized a hundred years ago.

During the last three decades, English women, most of them have had fair opportunities for good and happiness. That they have not made the most of these has been chiefly, I think due to a deficiency in education for women.

Women have not grasped the facts of life or the origins of evil and disease. Too many women call themselves fatalists and libel God with their misfortune.

It takes time, patience and commonsense to analyze the damage of war in the light of cause and effect. Women tend to be irresponsible and they will not take the trouble to do this.

Women before the war had no time to think and now, when they are doing their best to help the men in the prosecution of war, they still have no time to think.

The surplus of women in the fighting countries after the war, will be an evil which will be impossible to right. It is fatuous to speak of women's' place in the sun after the war. For thousands of women, the whole object in life, marriage and childbearing, will be nonexistent.

Some women will, of course be able to steer clear of an extremely vicious world and let their influence for good be felt. However, vice will again predominate, as it always has. This is the inevitable result of two great world wars.

The people who think and preach otherwise are merely those who dream of a foolish paradise. They pay no attention to the facts of the case.

Fighting, on the colossal scale of the present day, means degeneration on the same scale. Nature's scheme of things has been set in defiance and outraged. Men are suffering the intolerable injustice of death just as they reach the full vigor and strength of manhood.

Women must suffer in the years to come the same injustice of degeneration. Thousands of women will make the attempt to be their best, but nature will defeat them.

Nature intends most women to be wives and mothers. These are essential facts of life.

Men and women need the help of each other to attain to their best, mentally, morally and physically. Those who are celibate, or those who have relations with women (who are too socially scared to call their wives) miss that complete harmony which is life at its best.

Today as one moves along the streets, one catches one's breath in horror; everyone is in mourning for a lost friend or family member.

War on this gigantic scale means extermination of all that is good and fine in the nation. Mankind has outraged Nature and God. A bird's eye view of the world today would show man like an unreasoning child destroying everything, himself included.

Taking the large view of things, it is immaterial that the Allies are wholly in the right, that our cause is just, and that Germany was the aggressor. It is God's world we bring our children into. Man has spoiled it.

In the aftermath of war, when Europe's best manhood is buried or crippled, the men who are left alive, may not be the best and the brightest. Less good than the best will influence Europe, and people after a few years, forgetting the reasons for the injustice by which they are surrounded, will condemn human nature and say it has not improved.

'The Allies are determined to crush Germany. Germany is determined to crush the Allies.

The probability is that neither will accomplish their goal but thousands, millions, of additional lives will be wasted in the attempt.

This generation is imbued with the idea of self-sacrifice and is reconciled with the complete abnegation of the individual. But what of the present-day children, the babies that are now being born?

If this war continues with its vast consequences of evil, the belief that the accumulated force of immorality, disease and unnatural conditions will leave our children with no chance decent lives.

The infant mortality rate throughout the country has greatly increased during the past year. A baby in normal times had a normal birth, a normal mother and normal chances: things today are abnormal. The baby whose entire well-being depends on normal conditions, suffers as a direct consequence.

Prenatal conditions are stacked against a normal family life. Women are not blocks of wood. Those who are condemned through pregnancy to a life of inaction must suffer martyrdom through the anxiety for their partners. War brides are often changed to a life of uncertainty.

The disasters of war are liable to produce miscarriage and other abnormalities. In addition, the anxiety and horror of these times makes it impossible for many women to nurse their babies. The day of normalcy will return one day for women, but mothers and babies are heavily handicapped at the present time.

Ruskin accuses women, alluding to war:

"It is your fault, wholly yours. Only by your command, or by your permission, can any war take place. And the real final reason for all the poverty, misery and rage of battle throughout Europe, is simply that you women, however good, however religious or self-sacrificing are too selfish and too thoughtless to take pains for any creature out of your own immediate circle."

Women should have given a united and overwhelming support to the International Woman's Congress at the Hague.

Women should revolt at the continuation of the folly which is destroying Europe. For the sake of our children, I submit that it is a woman's duty to petition the governments of the belligerent countries for arbitration instead of war.

Arbitration should take the place of bloodshed. The arguments given against this are, I think, untenable. First that Germany must not be left with any strength of resistance. Second that our sacrifices must not have been in vain.

Germany's pugnacity and apparent belief in the psychological necessity for war will be curbed in future by the Hague Tribunal, supported as necessary by International force.

The men and boys, who have died, would rather that they had suffered and died in place of those others who still have God's gift of life.

Signed Charlotte E. Payne (nee Nixon)

Daughter Rhoda Concludes Her Biography
1950–51, Aged 71–73

Final chapter written by Rhoda Lawrence after Charlotte's Death in 1951.

In 1949 my sister, Iris, and her husband decided to give up renting Greyfriars from my mother. Their children were gown up and working in London which was the obvious place for them all to live.

After much discussion, we managed to persuade Mummy to put Greyfriars on the market. Basil had made his life in America and would never want to live there, and I had my own home in Essex. Greyfriars was far too big for her to live in alone, even had she been able to afford to do so.

The whole family was very relieved when she agreed to sell Greyfriars but depressed when she announced that nothing would induce her to take a penny less than 10,000 pounds. Owing to the war and consequent neglect the property had deteriorated and the

Charlotte at Greyfriars

chances of her ever getting such a large sum for it seemed very remote.

However, she was undaunted and completely determined, and announced her intention of moving into the house to live in two rooms as caretaker until such time as the house was sold.

Greyfriars was a very lonely house, surrounded by dark pine trees, and on one side, a vast expanse of desolate common land stretching for several miles; the nearest neighbour half a mile away in a cottage down the road which led to the house and went no further.

It was undoubtedly the most unsuitable place for an old lady with a very weak heart to live by herself; but it was hopeless to argue with my mother once she had made up her mind to do anything, and in the autumn of 1949 shortly after she had returned from Greece, she went back to live at Greyfriars.

One thing I made her promise me was that she would never sleep alone in the house. There was an old retainer in the village who agreed to arrive each evening at about 7:30 pm and leave next morning at 8 am.

Bino, my mother's youngest brother who lived in great discomfort on Salisbury Plain in an old crashed glider, spent much of his time during the winter months at Greyfriars. He was practically blind; he was no help and created a great deal of extra work for her.

Unfortunately, they disagreed upon every subject under the sun which resulted in rows. Often the row terminated in my uncle leaving the house abruptly. He would return to Salisbury Plain complaining bitterly that his nervous system had been completely upset and his digestion ruined.

1949 was a very cold winter and, owing to the need for stringent economy, the central heating boiler never lit. My mother used the kitchen as her living room and slept in the maid's room above.

She employed a gardener who, among many other things, did the chickens she insisted on keeping at the bottom of her garden. He also stoked the hot water boiler except on Sundays, when she did all this herself. An old retainer came in four hours a week to clean.

At that time my daughter, Verity, went to school at Godalming, so on the pretext of taking her out, I used to go down for a few weekends during the term. On these occasions Mummy would insist on lighting the heating boiler and doing all the cooking herself, as she always thought that all children were starved at boarding school, she would exhaust herself turning out wonderful meals for Verity.

It always took her longer than anyone else to prepare a meal as she took infinite trouble and sometimes lunch would be late. But when it arrived it was a chicken roasted to perfection with all the sauces and beautifully cooked vegetables, followed by Verity's favorite chocolate pudding.

Although those weekends were exhausting for Mummy, I think they made her feel that she was serving some other purpose at Greyfriars besides caretaking, and I know how much she loved having us there.

Unfortunately, although there were many things that I could have done to help, she never would allow it. "You have come to see Verity." She would say firmly "and you know I can't stand anyone else in the kitchen." When Monday morning came, and I had to return home I was depressed at the thought of leaving her there all alone and worried because she looked so tired.

That Christmas holidays, 1950, we took the children to Switzerland for two weeks holiday. There I had the misfortune to break my leg. I knew that Mummy was certain to hear of my accident and I dreaded to think of the anxiety that it would cause her.

Sure enough, after I had been in bed two days, a telegram arrived. "Can easily arrange for gardener to live in here. Can I come out and nurse you and bring you back when you are well enough to travel?" I hastily sent a wire back stating that my leg was nothing to worry about and that I was returning with the family in ten days' time.

I followed this up by sending her post cards each day until I left, reporting excellent progress and making as light of the leg as possible. The journey home was quite one of the longest and most painful that I have ever endured. I came the whole way on a stretcher, but each time that I was moved was agony.

When we eventually arrived at Victoria, I was an exhausted wreck. I shall never forget looking out of the window as the train drew up. There on the platform, her face contorted with worry, stood Mummy. My cheerful post cards had not convinced her and she'd made that long journey from Greyfriars to see for herself if I was alright.

I think the knowledge that there was someone there whose agony was even greater than mine made me pull together. I had a quick swig at the brandy flask in my pocket and, by the time she came into the carriage, I was once more able to make light of the situation.

From the suitcase that she carried in her hand it was obvious that she badly wanted to return with me to Essex by car that night to see me safely installed in my own bed. Unfortunately, by the time we had got all the luggage and the two children into the car, with me and my leg taking up the entire back seat, there was no room for her. She had to make that tiring journey back to Greyfriars in the dark. I am sure that it must have be midnight before she got home.

All through that spring and summer I was unable to drive a car and had to remain stationary owing to my leg. In the meantime, Mummy continued to work herself to the bone at Greyfriars. To my great relief in the early summer, she managed to find a German girl who wished to learn English and this girl, whose name was Hannah, went to live with her, proving herself to be a wonderful worker and a charming individual.

At the end of 1950, Mummy received an offer for the house. It was a few hundred short of the 10,000 and was immediately refused. Fortunately, the would-be buyers wanted the house very much and after a few weeks agreed to pay the necessary sum. Mummy was sad, as my brother Basil was returning to England in the summer and she had hoped that he and his family would be able to spend his leave at Greyfriars.

I think she had realized by this time that it was all too much. Her overdraft was increasing in the most alarming manner. The date of possession was the first of May, 1950; from then onwards Mummy would be homeless.

With this fact in view and with a certain amount of trepidation I approached my husband, Guy, and asked him if he would allow me to do up the cottage on the end of our house for her.

There were war evacuees in the cottage at the time and although I had often tried to get them out, I had not succeeded, and they had been there for ten years, since the beginning of the war. Guy hardly bothered to look up from the cross word puzzle he was doing at the time to answer. "She can have the cottage, but you will never get the evacuees out."

Fortunately, an almshouse in the village became vacant that week and I went to the evacuees and offered to pay half their rent if they would move into it. They accepted the offer and within the month they were out, and the painters and decorators were in.

The cottage was in a very bad condition and had no bathroom or electric light. A great many other things had to be done before Mummy could move in, but I thoroughly enjoyed planning it for her. It was most exciting as the cottage began to take shape.

One lovely day in March, I took all the children and Nanny to the point-to-point and were just finishing our picnic lunch when to my horror,

I saw Wyatt, our butler, who we had left at home, threading his way through the crowd and obviously searching for me. I knew that something ghastly must have happened.

At that moment he saw us and came hurrying across to the car to say that I must go at once to Mrs. Payne at Greyfriars who had had a stroke. No one has ever left a point-to-point so hurriedly or driven so far or so fast. All the way I was thinking about the lovely little cottage which in all probability Mummy would now never live in.

When I arrived at Greyfriars, the housekeeper, Hannah, told me that three days before my aunt Priscilla, Charlotte's sister, had been taken ill. Mummy had insisted on hiring a taxi and driving over to her at Newbury in the middle of the night. Since then she had been nursing her day and night without any rest.

My aunt Priscilla had rung up in the morning to tell Hannah about the stroke and my sister Iris, who fortunately was staying the night at Greyfriars, had gone over to Newbury in her car to bring Mummy home. They would be arriving any minute.

Poor darling Mummy. I had no idea what a stroke meant until I helped her out of the car that night. She could hardly speak, and her face was distorted on one side.

I put her to bed surrounded by hot water bottles and sent for the doctor. That night I slept in her room. Being back at Greyfriars seemed to do her good as she slept well and, in the morning, seemed much better.

She was absolutely furious at the idea that she had had a stroke and insisted that she had flu. There was no point in arguing so we forgot about the stroke which she had obviously had. In three days time her face and speech returned to normal and she appeared to have recovered. The doctor said that she must stay in bed for three weeks which she did and I, feeling much happier, returned to my home in Essex to continue superintending the work on the cottage.

On April 28, Mummy left Greyfriars for good. I am sure she must have felt overwhelmed by sadness at leaving the house that she had lived in so long and loved so much.

Unfortunately, the cottage was not quite finished and still smelt horribly of paint, so she moved into Guy and my house for a week before moving in. Possibly this was just as well as it meant that she had a good rest before starting to unpack and arrange things.

When the painters moved out at the end of the week, we were all ab-solutely delighted with the result of their labours. The cottage was really perfect, and Mummy was thrilled with it and immediately christened it "Luxury Lodge." As she wanted above all to be independent, after moving her in and filling her rooms with flowers, we left her to get on with her life while we got on with ours.

After all the work which she had been used to doing at Greyfriars, the cottage seemed far easier. Everything was electric. I provided her with eggs butter and vegetables and did all her shopping for her. My brother Basil, and his family, arrived from America and they all came down for the day to see her on their way to Frinton where they had taken a house for three months.

Everything was too good to be true. Mummy was very happy, loved being amongst her grandchildren, adored her cottage and seemed well. Three very contented weeks passed, then I had to go away for a week with my husband.

When I came back Mummy was obviously not at all well and told me that she had had a peculiar attack during my absence when she had been unable to move at all for about ten minutes. Luckily, she had been sitting in a chair at the time, so it had not mattered very much.

Two days later we had planned to go over to Frinton to spend the day with Basil. In the morning as I was dressing, the bell, which I had con-nected between my room and Mummy's in the cottage rang. It was under-stood between us that this only be rung in emergencies, so I pulled on my dressing gown and ran down the passage through the door that connected the house to the cottage.

She was in her bedroom looking very flushed and shaken. She had fallen over and, once again, she had been unable to move. She didn't think that she felt well enough to go to Frinton. I put her to bed and sent the doctor who took hours to come and eventually arrived at lunch time.

The doctor said that she must remain in bed a week and change her en-tire way of living. Breakfast in bed in the mornings and no exertion wha-tever...the life of an invalid from now on. The one thing poor darling Mummy hated was being a nuisance.

She thought that she was adding to my difficulties by being ill in the cottage and kept suggesting that she go to an old women's nursing home. I was adamant. Of course not, she must stay. We loved having her and if the worst came to the worst, she could have her own maid staying in the cottage as there was a spare room.

It was then that I really realized and appreciated the affection and devotion of my own staff, all of whom had been with me or my family for many years.

First Phyllis, the housemaid, came to me and offered to take Mummy all her food over on a tray from my house and to do all the necessary jobs to make her comfortable. Then Margaret, the cook, said that one more to cook for would make no difference in a household that already contained so many. Then Nanny, who had made the curtains in the cottage, said she could easily manage one more person's washing each week, and so it went on to Wyatt, who undertook to clean her shoes, then to Heinz, the cooks husband, asked if he could carry wood and coal into the cottage.

They all said, "Don't get a stranger to look after Mrs. Payne. She mightn't like her, and we would love to help her." Fortunately, Mummy already had a charming daily woman to work for her each morning in the cottage so there was no question of anyone having to do extra housework.

Once again, Mummy got better although she was never her old self again. My brother gave her a wonderful chair on wheels for the garden and she used it to sit in there all day by the herbaceous boarder while Lucinda played around her. She was determined to have her chair concealed by a large tree so that my husband, Guy, wouldn't see his mother-in-law every time he looked out of the house.

Luckily, it was a lovely summer and I stayed home as much as I could to be with her. I used to garden madly while she lay out in the sunshine watching me. It made me very sad to see how patiently she, who had always been so energetic, had taken to living the life of an invalid.

I am quite sure now that she knew she was dying but she hated worrying me and so kept it to herself. A month went by. Basil came over from Frinton quite often to see her. Mummy was getting all her money affairs settled and each time he came they talked about business matters. She was very worried in case he invested any of the Greyfriars money, which she had given him, in armament shares or anything connected with war.

At the end of July, the children came home from school and the holiday started in earnest. My time was so occupied with visits to dentists, horse shows and tennis tournaments that I am afraid that I did not think about Mummy as much as I should have.

She was feeling her heart a lot and was spending much of her time in bed. I could see that she was feeling worried about her condition, but she would not see the doctor and kept saying that no one could do anything for her as she was suffering from old age. About this time one of the children's horses got tetanus which caused me great anxiety.

Then Lucinda suddenly developed a high temperature and every symptom of polio. Fortunately, this turned out to be only a very bad attack of acidosis, but at the time I could think of little else.

When we had got over these worries, I took Dawn and Verity to Frinton to stay with Basil and play in the children's tennis tournament. The day we left she was in bed, but she assured us that she was feeling better and would be up the next day.

After two very exhausting days at Frinton, culminating in Verity winning the tournament with her cousin Johnnie Brooks, we returned to Little Easton on Friday afternoon.

I was delighted to see that Mummy was out in the garden once more and seemed to be in very good form. I remember taking a drink out to the garden and sitting on the end of her chair as I told her all about our adventures at Frinton. As usual she was tremendously interested in everything that had happened and happy to have us all back home again.

After a while she decided to go in and after she had gone, I started dead heading the sweet peas. This always took me some time and when I had finished, I was surprised to see that Mummy had come out again and was in her chair. It was such a lovely evening that she had decided to come out for a little longer.

I fetched myself another drink and we sat talking together until the sun went down. I remember being slightly bothered by her suddenly asking me if there was an undertaker in nearby Dunmow. Apart from that, our conversation was all about Basil and his children and other everyday matters. I helped her carry her blanket and books back to the cottage. I left her sitting in her armchair waiting for Phyliss to bring her meal on a tray.

The children went to bed early that night as they were tired having been at a dance the night before. I was sitting with Guy in the study when suddenly the telephone rang.

I heard Phyliss' voice at the other end speaking from the cottage asking me to come at once. I dropped the telephone and ran. Phyllis was holding Mummy down in her chair and as soon as I came in, I realized that she had no idea what she was doing or who I was.

Looking back, I realized there was much I might have done but, in that crisis, I lost my head and did the wrong thing. All the time she was fighting against Phyllis and me. She wanted to get out of the chair. It was as much as we could do to hold her there. I thought that she must have been having a violent heart attack and my first thought was brandy.

I poured some into a glass from a bottle always kept in the sitting-room. Twice she knocked it away but, when I had filled it the third time, she grabbed it and drained the glass. The doctor arrived and told me that brandy was the one thing she should not have had. He gave her an injection of morphia and carried her upstairs. We undressed her and put her to bed. The whole of her right side was paralyzed, and she had lost her speech. For me, Mummy died that Friday night, when she left my garden.

We sent for Basil, Iris and Priscilla and they all arrived about midnight. The doctor came again about 2 am and, after seeing Mummy, came down to tell us she would not survive the night unless he gave her an injection to stimulate her heart. I remember thinking that if she was never going to be able to move or speak again, she would sooner be dead. Basil wanted her to have it and persuaded me to agree. The next ten days were agonizing for us who loved Mummy. There was so much that she wanted to say, and we were too stupid to understand. August 17 was Priscilla's birthday and Mummy had always given her carnations on this day. There were not many out in the greenhouse, so I took some to add to a vase in Mummy's cottage.

When I gave them to Mummy to give to Priscilla, she very carefully removed two slightly withered ones from the bunch. The two very efficient nurses who had come down from London to look after her had told me that she was not really suffering much as she did not know what was going on. How wrong this proved to be. On August 18, Mummy had another stroke from which she never regained consciousness. Three days later she died. Her lifetime motto was:

217

"The world is my country, and to do good is my religion."

I found this written roughly inside one of my mother's notebooks. It was so entirely her creed in life that I am writing it here. Some people failed to understand her, but those who did realized that she was an outstanding character with unlimited strength in her own convictions and indomitable moral courage. She would not tolerate injustice. She had worn herself out during two world wars looking for the Truth and fighting public opinion.

POEMS

Passion about Death and the Folly of War

Poem: Dream to Death

If you would help me, when I die
Help me to forget to weep,
Let some most perfect music Lull my sad heart to sleep.
Music will swiftly bring to me
Peace. And with failing breath, I
Shall pass from pain to dream
And from dream to death.

Poem: Evil

Evil, Evil?
What is Evil?
There is only one Evil
To deny Life.

Poem: Once, were Youth and Men (by D.H. Lawrence)

War came, and every hand raised to murder,
Very, good, very good, every hand raised to murder,
Very good, very good, I am murderer!

It is good, I can murder and murder, and see them fall
The mutilated, horror-struck youths, a multitude
One on another, and then in clusters together,
Smashed, all oozing with blood and burned in heaps
Going up in fetid smoke to get rid of them
The murdered bodies of youths and men in heaps
And heaps and heaps and horrible reeking heaps
Till it is almost enough,
Thousands and thousands of gaping, hideous foul dead
That once were youths and men.

Poem: The Peace Crank (About Charlotte in WW I)

Who thinks that Death is a hideous fraud?
And Life the one thing to applaud,
Who'd kiss the feet of Mr. Ford,
The Peace Crank.

Who says sans reason and sans rhyme,
That war is the most heinous crime,
Calls for arbitration all the time,
The Peace Crank.

Who says without a trace of mirth?
That Empire, honour, nothing's worth
The Hell that war has made on earth.
The Peace Crank.

Who treats with unremitting scorn?
Our world that we shall see reborn
A better world, from days forlorn,
The Peace Crank.

Poem: Christmas 1915 The Stupidity of War

The world is better for their sacrifice,
No man is better if he kills his brother,
For him is left remembrance of despair.
And if he lives and wishes to keep sane
He makes himself less man and far more beast.
Those murdered men today on either side
Have killed the minds of those who have not died,
A ruined world has cost us too much
Our gallant buried youth and youth turned evil.

Poem: New Year 1916 Our Duty is to the Living

The dead are dead, our duty is to the living,
We cannot give them back what they have lost,
Poor dead,
But boys still stand bright eyed and fearless,
And let us strive, that peace may come
Before they, too, are stiffened corpses
Rotting in the sun and wet and filth
Corrupting God's good world.
For Christ's sake Peace.
Our duty is to the living

Poem: 1917 England Died with You

This, which once was England, now is hell
And all its people fiends, bewitched by war,
The lust for blood has seared and marred their souls,
Reason betrayed and sin holds carnival
What is the magic in this world of war?
That every crime is sanctioned in its name
And men are conscious, still and unashamed?

221

Women, the Church and even the world's great men
Who should have stood for Truth and all it means,
Now clamour that they gladly sacrifice
For King and Country other peoples' lives.
Oh, splendid youth, by self-made saints betrayed
Sometimes you fought for England,
And England died with you.

From the Daily Mail Newspaper in July 1915

"An unknown Canadian was seen standing and wounded on a German parapet, he hurled had thrown every bomb he carried, weeping with rage, hurled bricks and stones, until his end came."

Poem: (For An Unknown Canadian)

When he knew that death was certain
He wept with bitter rage.
Before it had seemed a lesser thing.
These wars, which great men wage.
The sun shone down with splendor
On a world divinely fair,
And himself, he was the compliment
Of that life which he should share.
He visualized the horror and death
Before they struck him down,
And he thought of women, whose life he was
In his far away hometown.
He hardly saw those Germans
Whom he strove to kill and maim.
For tears of despair had blinded his eyes
At the failure of Life's game.

Poem: In Memorial for My Sister, Priscilla (Gladys, Lady Stalbridge)

Each wreath's thought, which on the coffin lies.
Before one feels again the throb of life.
Fast beating through the days and dries one's eyes.
We give one day to you and sorrows knife
Cuts deep. We think and know what we have lost,
We feel your presence, hear your voice and weep,
We think of days long gone by and count the cost
Of a lost friend. Sad harvest now we reap
Of things undone, and, life holds less for these
Who were your friends, although they hardly knew,
How much you meant to them till Death's repose?
Had wrapped you close, and, then the knowledge grew.
Each wreath's a thought, which on the coffin lies
Before again to life we turn our eye.

Poem: Titanic Disaster. A Thought for the Dead

Life is finished and its scope is over,
One moment more, and I with all my hopes
Of better things will be beneath the gloom
Of rushing waters, the waves unheedful,
Will roll on like Time and Tide relentless.
And even you, who loved me more than life,
As I do you, will forget. Goodbye.

Poem: (For Edward and Eddy Killed while Flying September 23, 1929)

When those we know who have been much alive,
Full of keen valor, laughter, love of life,
With confidence in youth and in themselves,
When they most suddenly, disastrously

Are dead; it seems it cannot be for they
Are here beside us and we see them still,
War, keen and in their youth, all conquering
They stay with us some hours, a day, a week,
And then they fade and vanish into mist.
Poor ghosts! Unjust, most tragic and unfair
That they are ghosts and not the men they were.

Poem: For Puck Grosvenor, Charlotte's Nephew (Killed in plane crash flying across Australia)

All the while and for all time
In broken hearts he lives,
Blue eyes smiling, guileless youth
Striving for the best and Truth,
A gay and very gallant youth
Radiance of hope and laughter.
Gambling on his life – and dying
In the miracle of flying,
Life defeated by disaster.
If only he could have foreseen
The death in life his death would mean
All the while and for all time in broken hearts he lives.

Poem: The Tale is Told (The Degradation of War)

The tale is told, alas! the tale is told.
Chapter and verse it's through – and, we are old.
Great faith we had in life and laughter
Now dead sea fruit, we look back after
All the happenings of these heartbreak years
And see ourselves frustrated. Death and tears
And sorrow – and, the suicide of war
Its great injustices – we can laugh no more.

Far better not to have been born, than know
The degradation, war makes man endure
This tragedy of living.

Poem: Overture to War 1936

The hearts of men are breaking
In anguish – dully aching.
Man's been his own unmaking
Through centuries of pain
And today the air is humming
With the word that war is coming
And men's heart cry despairing
"For Christ's sake not again!"
Can there be no escaping
This crime that's in the making
The present, future staking.
On war. The Devil's plan.
At night the horror grips us
And at morning, first awakening
The hearts of men are breaking
At man's cruelty to man.

Poem: Change of Heart April 1939

We'll give to God his due and plan
A better world for martyred man.
Peace and Goodwill shall play their part
In universal chance of heart.
The clamour of armaments should cease
In a world resolved to live in Peace.
To fill one's home with tuneless laughter
Today is sacrilege, after
The murder and martyrdom of Spain.

Thousands on both sides have died in vain,
And women's torture, tears and pain
Have helped arms firms to quickly gain
Colossal wealth and some can smile
When dividends roll in the while.
A change of heart. Let's fling aside
Can't and humbug and decide
That Life is Truth and Truth is life
That we can put an end to strife
By immediate bloodless sacrifice
Offer our wealth in place of lives
To right the wrongs of the world –
A change of heart. This is God's plan
Heaven on Earth for every man.

Poem: The Spinsters, 1937

Supposing that it should come.
That nothing goes, according to plan.
That even gas masks are not used
What becomes of us?
All this wasted energy
And no kudos – V.A.D's. and W.A.A.C's
No happy days and no adventure,
We'd given our lives for Britain and a War.

Poem: Colonel Blimp (Charlotte on English Decision Makers)

Of course, Old Boy, we've made a packet
But there's a chance Peace may gain ground
And end the racket,
Perpetual Peace, it is absurd
An insult to the white man's world.

Poem: The Prime Minister, The Wartime Appeaser 1939

Chamberlain, the Man of Peace
Who made all plans for war
And overlooked no detail
To maintain the Empire's tradition
He would not consider even the Van Zeeland Report
Which, would definitely have cleared the road for Peace.
He bowed politely and made no further comment
When a great petition was given, to urge a conference.
And refusing George Lansbury and other Christians
When they also pleaded for this conference,
He pledged his word to give Poland military assistance
To resist Hitler's demand, "Justice for Germany."
Chamberlain, the Man of peace,
God help his victims, the Youth of Europe.

Poem: Knaves and Fools (War to Save Face?)

The bankruptcy of Statesmanship
In the hands of knaves and fools,
And all the folk of England
And those where Hitler rules
Condemned to death and blood and sweat
Because of knaves and fools.
Must we all be blind to conscience
And accept this hideous fraud.
Dangling a little gas mask
To show we're in accord
With Chamberlain and Halifax
And the nauseating hordes
Of those self-righteous people
Who see virtue in the sword.
Sophistication has its rules

And so like sheep, we go
To slaughter and be slaughtered
Although the Truth we know.
The knaves and fools have made this war.
Each conscript must be tame,
And Chamberlain, to save his face
Gives Hitler all the blame.

Poem: Save Our Souls (SOS What can we do?)

What can we do when the world's askew?
And the end no one can foretell,
When the boys are dead, and reason fled,
And blood has made the crowds see red,
What can we do in this hell?

What can we do when they seem so few?
Who can sift real Truth from the lies?
Of Government, Press and the wireless
The refugee's and hideous mess
Of war – and youth's stifled cries?

What can we do in this devil's stew?
Of crime which our leaders have made,
Setting a pace in an armaments race,
Faking a Cause and misstating a Case,
What, in God's name, can we do?

Poem: I Accuse (So Many of Lying and Deceit, December 1939)

J'Accuse:
The Prime Minister of a gross political blunder
"The offer of military assistance to Poland"
The Government of defeating Peace by every means in

Its power and of making war its sole objective
Labour Leaders of the betrayal
Of their Party and Principles
Press and wireless of lying,
War mongering propaganda.
The Financiers for supporting
A campaign of commercialized murder
The People for their apathy and
Consequent consent to the greatest crime in the history of the world.
Signed: A. Citizen, September 1939

Poem: Indictment of War Mongers 1914 to 1918

To save their prestige, armour proper and pride
Ten million died.
To back their tortuous twists of argument
No death they went.
To prop the structure better hands had built
Your blood they spilt.
A generation dead and now again,
High sounding phrase and
Glib half Truth have failed,
Ambition chants its murderous refrain
Youth to the cross of sacrifice once more is nailed.
It will be ever so, until youth's call
I heard the sickening screams of strife
Youth of the Nations,
Join, once brothers all.
None can deny you, life

Poem: The Missing Generation

The missing generation
At long last, its loss is felt.

For men are vainly calling
For a leader to defend
Their right to life and living
And their will to ask when this war shall end.

Poem: Save Us from Those Evil Things

God in heaven help us,
Save us from evil things,
From Halifax and Chamberlain,
From death their folly brings.
Save us from the lying press
From the unctuous B.B.C.
And from the self-righteousness
That allows these things to be.
Help all men proclaim this Truth –
War's tyranny supreme,
Has shattered youth's brief hope of life
That dream within a dream.
There is no reason for this crime,
This nightmare world of sorrow,
That bids all men obscenely kill,
And cancels their tomorrow.
God in heaven help us,
Save us from these evil things,
From Chamberlain and Halifax,
And the death their folly brings.

War, Death and Sacrifice

Poem: Signature Tune (Of a Generation Condemned to Death)

A quarter of a century has gone,
Again, a generation shares the fate
Of that one "missing," whom we still should mourn,
Their wisdom might have saved the world from hate.
Dear Youth, so guileless, gallant, full of hope,
You could not know that men would be so base
For their foul ends, to use all means to dope
The easy credence of the populace.
And these cry now, most lustfully, for blood
To feed their virtue. War is a crusade:
And death comes swift in overwhelming flood.
Your lives are forfeit. The debt must be paid.
Youth betrayed. Hopeless, singing on your way
That each "tomorrow is a lovely day."

Poem: British Public Opinion October 1940

Britain blinded by false virtue
And the evil lust for killing,
God and men will not forgive us
For this orgy of blood spilling.

Poem: Civilization (The Bombs Come Shrieking Down, 1940)

The children come from the country,
The children come from the town,
But wherever they go in England
The bombs come crashing down,

Of what are the women thinking
That crimes like these can be,
And what are the women doing
To stop this agony.

Our gay, defenseless children,
Look trusting to the sky,
But in Germany and England
It is decreed – they die.
No man will say a word to save
The children from their fate –
Germans and English from the air
Drone down their hymn of hate.

For crimes as dastardly as these
We never can atone.
The evil working in our midst
From strength to strength has grown.
From the depths of God's blue ether
The bombs come shrieking down
On children from the country,
And children from the town.

Poem: Morale (Morale is a Manipulated Affliction)

Morale is an affliction,
Callous – cruel indifference
To the suffering of others.
The radio, the press,
Colonel Blimp and hard baked spinsters
Suffer from this affliction.
People of goodwill – normal people,
Mothers, children.
The youth of all lands
Hate the obscenity of War.
They pray for Peace.

Poem: For the Independent Labour Party (I.L.P.) and the Peace Pledge Union (P.P.U.)

A humanitarian
Can have no axe to grind
His goal must be
To end war.
To stop it,
To save young men
Overwhelmed by disaster
And the monstrous
Injustice of death
And the children,
Frightened, frantic children
Smothered under bricks and rubble
Buried under steel and concrete.
And some drowned like rats
In deathtrap shelters.
And others burning,
Burning fiercely
Their soft, white flesh
Like tallow candles.
A humanitarian
Can have no axe to grind.
His goal must be
To end war,
To STOP IT.

Poem: Negotiate Peace (Stop This Folly: Stop This Crime)

Stop this folly: Stop this crime,
Stop bombing children for all time
Stop incensate, obscene killing.
Stop this blood lust; Hate distilling
Primitives now lead the Nation,

233

Spinsters nurtured in frustration
And every ego thrusts itself
Into the orb of righteousness.
Philanthropists and able men
Proclaim by speech, proclaim by pen,
After the war the world will be
A heaven of love and equity,
A world of charity and laughter.
The war worthwhile for this hereafter.
But they forget that not again
Can life be given to the slain.
The conscience of the world is dead
Primeval instinct rules instead.
The politicians murder youth,
They have to camouflage the Truth.
They dress it in a deadly glamour,
The press and radio then clamour,
The people doped, bewildered, dumb,
Cannot be heard above this hum.
They know that victory, nothing's worth.
The hell that war has made on earth.
The Church and State their chorus swell,
Telling the people all is well.
With this world of their unmaking,
The myriad hearts now breaking
Cry to God, "How long? How Long?"

Poem: Churchillian Ode (Charlotte's Bete Noir 1941)

Missing generations
Leave no leaders
They are dead
And instead
A Monster.

His decrees,
Obscenities
Why should we die,
You and I
By his decree?
Free the bandage
From your eyes.
Sacrifice
Is wanton lust
The price of gold
To behold.

Poem: A Nation of Cads

The Englishman in great self-righteousness
Scorns Truth and Reason and all common sense.
Blinded by fatuous pride and arrogance
He presumes honour in war's circumstance
His ignorance of fact, makes argument
To human suffering and affliction
His own virtue is his one conviction,
With pompous condescension he deplores
There are sane men who will not kill in wars,
In youth's agony and crucifixion
His sunshine mind feels no contrition,
Women and children, he condemns to death
Cries "No Appeasement" with his fulsome breath
And "Victory."

Quotations: Far from Home by R H. Newman (1929)

"Let us remember further that for those who have not yet lived their young lives; there is nothing worse than dying."

"People wanted to be happy, they tried so pathetically hard"
"There was nothing they resisted with such determination as the impulse to anything seriously."

Poem: Post War Generation (Both Wars Were So Bright)

Decide, decide,
End fratricide,
Too many have died
With eyes open wide,
Committed suicide.
Alas, for this generation
They are conventional.
They would not speak the Truth,
And would not learn the Truth
Truth was to them anathema,
They would rather die, than know the Truth,
And they have died.
Alas, for this generation
And their painted world
Both wars were so bright

Poem: The Truth (And They Supplied, 1943)

Some years ago, in America
The Industrial Depression.
It must be remedied.
And so, they supplied
China and Japan with armaments
With equal zest.

But that was not enough
And Arabs and Jews in Palestine.
The Civil War in Spain,
These orders infinitesimal.
A world blackout
Was necessary.
To encompass – The highest peak
Of their endeavors
Fifty-two million per day on armaments.
Riches above the dreams of avarice,
And the blackout continued.

The conscience of the world was dead.
And youth, pathetic youth
Danced to the music that they played
And never questioned,
That the world's loss was irretrievable.
The unlived lives,
And the triumph of the lies,
Everywhere.

Stupidity of War

**Poem: Synopsis of War (Arrogance and War
Ignored by Powerful, Stupid People)**

Arrogant old men,
Insular minded old men
In power.
Glamorous women
Glittering with diamonds
And precious stones,
Thinly veiled limbs in chiffon

Scented and sensuous
Faces thick coated in powder and cosmetics,
Claw like, bloody fingered nitwits,
Each brain a vacuum.
Missing generations and empire
Mates are hard to find.
And old men in power
Can put on women, like coats on velvet,
And listen appreciatively
As they lap up the cream of contentment,
A war.

Insular minded, arrogant old men
Become valiant hearted,
And the women neurotic.
They chirp of honour
And clamour against peace at any price,
Whatever this may mean.
The price of peace is known
And can be calculated,
But the price of war is incalculable.
The loss of one life
And what it might have accomplished
Living for the glorification of God.
The potential greatness in men.
Christ, Beethoven, Shakespeare, Socrates
The incalculable loss to the world
Of lives unlived.
Sinister forces, abnormal forces
Vested Interests, armaments, profits,
Frustrated spinsters
Failures and futilies,
All working with evil intent
In the interests of war
The plot well hatched, made foolproof.

Arrogant old men, insular minded
And the neuroses of women.
A military guarantee to Poland.
A declaration of War against Germany.
The plot damnably planned
By a conscienceless few
Is set in motion.

Their bluff called
The old men, pained and surprised
Call to heaven their justification
And wallow in a sea of self-righteousness.
The forces of iniquity band together.

Arrogant old men, insular minded old men
In power,
Cancel out Truth and Reason
And the most monstrous crime in history
Becomes a Holy Crusade.

The conflagration,
Spreading, flaming,
Burning up youth,
The despairing heart of youth
And youth's lost hope
In life and life's endeavor.
Youth condemned to death
Youth cheated, crucified,
Youth exploited
In the great racket of war.
A chorus of fiends chanting,
The Press the Radio,
The neurotic women,
"Fighting for Freedom."
Politicians become spiritual leaders.
No cost too high for victory.

Children taken from mothers,
Scattered irresponsibly,
Tragedies innumerable from this dispersal.
Millions of homes wrecked,
And the insanity of high explosive
Thudding down and crushing
The lives and homes of humans.
Bombs shattering, burning
Human bodies –
Lovely bodies of girls and children
Charred to cinders.
Children buried alive, burned alive
Dying in indescribable torture.
Men firefighting,
Trapped roasted in flames
Their flesh frying
And still conscious.
Dogs and cats in the conflagration,
Faithful friends
Amazingly bewildered.

And in smug preparation for this disaster
Before the Declaration of War
These dumb ones slaughtered in millions
Friends of man suffering all torment.
Only in anguished eyes,
Remonstrance
At their great betrayal,
Dumb and uncomprehending
Of the madness of our world.
The reaction of the British people
In September 1939,
Stupefaction, bewilderment
Minds turned in,
To matters of infinitesimal importance,
Football pools, Cinema stars

Stupendous ignorance of fact
And political reality.
The upper social strata,
The privileged few
Privileged to know the Truth
Purr their contentment,
At the Government's
Code of honour and irresponsibility.
Two million surplus women,
Frustrated women,
Their frustration magnified
By a Declaration of War.
Competitive women, married and unmarried
All striving for the attention of the male.
Their minds preoccupied
By the niceties of perm
And the beatitude of beauty culture.
These hordes of women
Gaily into dress uniform
To take their place and form contact at long last
With men.
The upper social strata,
The privileged few,
Now lead the way.
Their opportunity for folly – limitless.
And all sources of power at their disposal.
Tragedy follows tragedy, disaster follows disaster,
Life defeated by death.
"Brave and modest men" die unprotestingly,
At the behest of the proletariat.
The people satiated with blood and murder,
Their minds embittered with sense of loss and horror.
A bogus hero leads the nation
From crime to greater crime.
In vainglorious frenzy,
Churchill denounces Peace, refutes Peace,

Embroils country after country
In massacre and death.
And fastens his own blood guilt
On a man less evil than himself, Opposition is defeated.
Efforts for Peace are barren and abortive.
The interests of humanity are sidetracked, forgotten,
Only politicians and important people
In varying paroxysms of virtue
Each grinding his own axe
For a specious brand of Utopia,
After the war – after the war!

Liberal Labor Party (L.L.P.) Amendment: December 1940 Suggested Conference for Peace discussions – supported by only six members of Parliament in 1941

At Westminster the rats, they scurry in and out
They've made war and only they know what it is about.
In Westminster, there are six men and all the rest are yellow.
Yellow rats, brown rats some very timid female rats
And one debauched fellow,
Debauched by blood. Debauched by crime,
He yelps Victory all the time.
Other species, there, are lurking
Worms pink, lush and mellow
Harold Nicholson to wit – Eden and Baker
Do their bit
They wallow, in the slime.

Washington: January 28, 1941. The President of the United States

"Congress must weigh seriously the question, whether it wants Great Britain, Greece and China to continue to fight. If this Bill does not pass, they cannot continue to fight."

Salvation for the Peoples of England, China, Greece,
If the U.S A. declines to pay,
This holocaust must cease,
The wily politicians all their guarantees unpaid
See the Peace and War Aims shattered,
Of their grim crusade.
An economic blizzard of magnitude immense
Makes freedom loving countries at long last see, Common Sense.
Salvation for the Peoples of England, China, Greece,
If Congress does not pass this Bill.
Thank God, we shall have Peace.

Poem: Summer 1941: (The Pinnacle of Destruction)

Today stark horror fills one's heart
God's world is one vast tomb.
Each one of us has failed to save
The people from their doom.
Dead men can never live again,
Creation is despoiled,
And only fools can hope remake,
A world by fools destroyed.

Poem: The Satyr (The Male of Greek Wartime Mythology Who Has It All)

His eyes glint with satisfaction,
He's grossly overfed,

His life is the reaction
To millions of the dead –
Girls and lovely women
Flatter and caress,
There's no one else
And half a loaf
Is better than no bread.
He's overworked. He has to cope
With feminine desire
But the world's a paradise
Of sex, to the Satyr.

Poem: Looking Back (Charlotte's Remembrances of War and Propaganda)

On the platform,
Mouthing honor and irresponsibility,
The ugly fierce one
Eyes grimly flashing.
Her rugged face
Like a rook, wave beaten,
Beaten by resentment,
And animosity.
Wisps of grey hair, limply shaking
All In a turmoil
Of military ardour
To shatter the white tranquility of Peace.

One cannot organize the people
Thousands and thousands
From every door and in every street
They swarm like ants
Darting hither and thither
All vastly preoccupied
With personal interest

Only lies can be organized.
Spread wholesale,
Blared from the radio
Every newspaper and newsreel
Coldly lying lies – lies – lies
Everywhere,
Truth lost in a fetid mass of lying propaganda.

Regiments of women Clucking like geese,
And the Church lying
Plausibly lying.
The youth of the world
Dying, dying.
And civilization in ruins
Crashing, crashing
Crashing at our feet
In this vortex
Of insanity
Barbarians
Blithely proclaim "New Orders"
For those living
Whom they're killing
Night and day,
Disastrous hour
Men in power
Have made this chaos,
Defeated God – and wrecked
The tranquility
Of order
Which is Peace

Poem: Creed (Charlotte's Belief)

The purpose of the world is Life,
The purpose of Life is the World.

Man's purpose is to be and do his best
Mentally, physically, morally –
For Life's sake and The World's
And in gratitude to God.

Poem: Corollary (The Antithesis of Her Belief)

The world is full of peoples, who scoffingly deplore
The use of life and wonder what God has made us for
To satisfy their foolish needs.
Kind men, invent a host of creeds
And talk about a soul.

Wrapping up
Charlotte's Collection of Poetry

Poem: Never Again (Charlotte's Battle Cry)

Never again the lies,
The lies that are heard on the air.
Never again let us read the lies,
The lies that are made to ensnare.
Never again let our lovely ones
Function as W.A.Fs and W.R.E.Ns,
They vamp for the guns,
These lovely ones
With never a thought for the men.
Never again, damnation
In a world where the sun should shine,
And never again a ration
Instead of good food and wine.
Never again let Government swine
Make and declare a war.

They have filched our lives
With their ideals and crimes, Never, never again.

Chorus. Never again a war obscene
Destroying all that might have been
Never again,
Never, never again.

Note across the side of the page, Charlotte has written
"Play to Tchaikovsky's piano concerto"

Poem: Wings of Death (Have Robbed the World of Virtue)

This monstrous death machine that man has made,
So sinister it's evil, unashamed
And unafraid boys hurl down death and smile
The while, seemingly, they do not know how vile
And dastardly they are. These wings of death
That drone above, to rob us of the breath
Of life. Foul devastation of the world.
Grim desecration of the will of God.
This obscene monstrous thing that man has made
For self-destruction and the good of trade.
Destroy, destroy, each boy and each machine
And each will he it had never been.
Money to burn and laughter from disaster,
Wings of death – fly faster, ever faster.
The world is now the mortuary of youth
Who should have lived to make our Heaven here?
Supreme injustice all their work undone.
Their lives unlived – before they had begun.
It needs the sense of years to understand
One's conscience and the evil that is planned
The tyranny of war;
These Things of Death
Have robbed the world of virtue and the
Breath of Life.

247

Poem: The Children (Reply to a Critical Newspaper Article)

No faith is left
In creed or policy,
Our goal must be met
To end this war,
To atop it.
To save young men
Overwhelmed by disaster
And the monstrous
Injustice of death.
To save the children,
Frightened, frantic children
Smothered under bricks and rubble,
Buried under steel and concrete.
Some drowned like rats,
In death trap shelters.
Others have burnt
Burnt fiercely,
Their soft, white flesh Like tallow candles.
No faith is left
In creed or policy
Our goal must be
To end this war,
To stop it.
Signed: Charlotte Evelyn Nixon-Payne, Northam, North Devon.

Poem: When (He Cried and Shot Himself to Death)

When the battle's smoke had lifted,
After the cannons roar had passed,
There arose a human being
For he the very last.
He smoothed his muddy uniform,

He raised his bloody head,
And sniffed the sanguine atmosphere,
When all around lay dead.
A ragged poster flapped at him,
He strained his falling sight,
"Your freedom is in danger"
"Defend with all your might."
My freedom is in danger,
He sadly shook his head,
"I've done too much for freedom now"
He cried and shot himself stone dead.

Poem: A Twilight Prayer for Young Christians

Charlotte did not want to Fight Wars for any Person or Cause, although this Poem Seems Anti-Semitic 70 years Later, I Doubt She was. Ikey Mo was in 1940s English slang for Jew

Yes! Ikey Mo forever!
I beg Thee, as I go,
God, keep him safe from wars afar.
Propping his paunch 'gainst cocktail bar
Stuffing his Blond with caviar,
Lighting at length his fat cigar,
My dear; my Ikey Mo.

The Germans do not like him,
But I dislike the Germ,
So, to my death I gladly go
To save poor outraged Ikey Mo.
Yes! Israel forever!
Cried with my latest breath.
Oh God I trust in you to see
That Mo, who hates them same as me
Won't suffer through death!

Index

CPSIA information can be obtained
at www.ICGtesting.com
Printed in the USA
FSHW011556270421
80739FS

9 780970 137456